MOVING YOUR FAMILY OVERSEAS

Rosalind Kalb & Penelope Welch

INTERCULTURAL PRESS, INC.

First published by Intercultural Press. For information contact:

Intercultural Press, Inc.
PO Box 700
Yarmouth, Maine 04096 USA
207-846-5168
Fax: 207-846-5181
www.interculturalpress.com

Nicholas Brealey Publishing
36 John Street
London WC1N 2AT, UK
44-207-430-0224
Fax: 44-207-404-8311
www.nbrealey-books.com

Book design by Patty J. Topel
Cover design by LetterSpace
Art concept by Penelope Laiton
Illustrations by Peter Bernard

Printed in the United States of America

04   03   02   01   00   8   9   10   11   12

Library of Congress Cataloging-in-Publication Data

Kalb, Rosalind C.
    Moving Your Family Overseas.
    p.   cm.
    Includes bibliographical references.
    ISBN 1-877864-14-5
    1. Moving, household.   2. Americans—Foreign countries.
I. Welch, Penelope A.   II. Title.
TX307.K35   1992
648'.9—dc20   92–21000
                                                            CIP

MOVING
YOUR FAMILY
OVERSEAS

Dedication

To our own families—John, Johanna, and Alex Kalb; and John, Tony, and Alex Welch—who learned along with us; and to all the other families who made our overseas experiences so interesting, exciting, and filled with friendship.

Contents

Acknowledgments

We are grateful to all the people who read the initial manuscript of *Moving Your Family Overseas* and brought our thoughts to life with their personal experiences: Lisa Benson, Alyce Boster, Pam and Jerry Casler, Mark Cohen, Wendy and Fred Endelman, John Kalb, Johanna Kalb, Barbara Maletz, Sue Ready, Ellen and Bill Roberts, Sharon and Bill Vipond, John Welch, and Sally and John Williams.

We also want to thank Brian Billow, Virginia McKay, Lillimore Mollin-Parker, Rose Ong, and Ronald Raymond for their suggestions and encouragement, and Milton and Rowna Cohen for their editorial assistance.

Introduction

Living overseas is an experience like no other. It is an opportunity to see the world from a new perspective and to live in a culture unlike your own. It is a chance to meet people who seem different from you though they are similar in many ways, and who seem like you even when they are very different. It is an occasion to grow, to develop new ideas and interests, and to try a new and interesting life-style.

It is also a time to have fun. We know because we have done it. We've floated in a junk on the South China Sea, lived with rice farmers in rural Japan, attended Ascot in the Royal Enclosure, eaten witchetty grubs in the Australian outback, welcomed Santa Claus on elephant back in Thailand, and spoken Japanese with our children over the dinner table. In a total of six overseas assignments, we have shared with our husbands and children many of the experiences and feelings described in this book. We have also shared with each other the frustrations of career adjustments and the challenges of maintaining families overseas. Much of the information in these chapters comes out of our personal experiences. The rest is the collected wisdom of a number of families living in many different parts of the world. The decision to write this book was the result of a growing appreciation of the pleasures and stresses of over-

Living overseas is a chance to see the world from a new perspective.

seas life and of the spirit of adventure which tempts families to explore the new and different. We hope the book will ease the way for your family by filling in any gaps in the information provided by your company or organization, and increase your enjoyment of the adventures which lie ahead.

Each family's experience will be unique, as will the experience of each family member, with different joys and problems. There is no one correct way to experience an overseas move. So, we have not written a how-to manual for overseas living (see Recommended Readings for books that give more specific detail). We offer instead a look at the challenges which face the family moving overseas and suggestions on how families can meet the challenges involved.

The book is divided into four sections. The first deals with the factors which should be considered in a family's decision to move overseas. The second looks at the process of adjusting to an unfamiliar culture and describes how individual family members may react to the changes in their lives. The third section describes some of the ongoing issues involved in maintaining family life overseas. The fourth focuses on the unforeseen complexities of the transition back home or to another country. Each phase of the move will bring new challenges: most will be stimulating and fun, while some may seem quite difficult or overwhelming. We hope they will all be as exciting for you as they have been for us. This book is not meant to scare you, but it does preview many of the uncertainties and concerns which families face in relation to their overseas assignment.

Uprooting your family to begin life in a new country is a complicated process. The book will prove most useful to you if you read it in its entirety prior to going on assignment. Reading about the experience in advance can provide several benefits for your family. First, you will be able to make a more informed and realistic decision about accepting or rejecting the assignment. The glamour and excitement of a potential move to a foreign country may cloud a family's judgment. You may hear only about travel opportunities, exotic life-styles, or generous living allowances but never about the extra stresses and strains which such a move can put on you and your loved ones. Making an educated decision about the move overseas will reduce the number of unwelcome surprises and will maximize your enjoyment of the experience.

The second important benefit is that preparation prior to leaving allows you to plan for the very best while still being prepared for whatever else may occur. Knowledge of potential difficulties will help you spot them early and handle them more effectively. We hope that knowing the possible stresses of overseas life will encourage you to talk them over within your family and with other families you meet abroad. Some of the greatest strains experienced by family members come from the false perception that no one else feels similar worries, pressures, or concerns. You can provide effective support for one another simply by discussing some of these feelings.

Reading this book during premove preparation can also help you make the best use of the choices available to you. In our experience, people cope most effectively and enjoy themselves most when they feel in control of their own lives. The degree to which people feel in control often has to do with the ability to choose the major directions in which their lives flow. For many families, the foreign assignment is the sought-after experience of a lifetime. For others, it is the only means of receiving a paycheck. Obviously, the overseas experience will not be the same for all families and may well be extremely different. One goal of this book is to help families recognize and maximize the choices that are available to them. Families for whom the move is not a free choice will need to work harder to identify other ways of expressing themselves—the neighborhood they select to live in; the kind of housing they obtain; the schools, house decor, or recreational activities they choose—in order to preserve their sense of personal control. Throughout this book we will try to highlight the situations in which important choices can be made so that you can select the options most beneficial to you.

Moving Your Family Overseas is directed primarily at families in which it is the husband's job which takes the family overseas. While there is a growing number of families on assignment because of the wife's occupation, that number is still relatively small. Therefore, with apologies to anyone we are slighting, we will usually be speaking of the husband as the employee and the wife as the spouse.

PART I

Deciding and Preparing to Move Overseas

one

What This Move Means for Your Family

When the boss offers an overseas transfer, what are the factors which you need to consider in making your decision? You may respond, "Decision—what decision? If I don't make this move, I'm out of a job. So what's the choice?" It is true that most job transfers don't come in the form of a choice. However, companies spend vast sums to maintain a family overseas, and they want, whenever possible, to avoid the added expense of bringing home a family that cannot make the adjustment to living in a foreign country. Therefore, it is important for yourselves, as well as for the company, to evaluate honestly and accurately your suitability for an overseas assignment.

At any given time, each family member is in a different place in his or her life. What is advantageous for one may not be advantageous or even desirable for another. Your task is to try to assess the impact that a foreign assignment will have on each person in your family and on the family system as a whole. Families find this process most stressful when the foreign transfer is required or important for the breadwinner's career but conflicts with the needs of other family members. Therefore, your first task is to find out as much as possible about the job and its future implications.

CAREER IMPLICATIONS OF THE NEW JOB

Before accepting an assignment overseas, try to get as accurate a picture as you can of the new job. Overseas employment often involves a great deal of business and professional travel, long working hours, and frequent entertaining. These may be exactly the stimulating and exciting aspects of the assignment which you are anticipating. On the other hand, many families find that the demands of the job far exceed anything they have experienced in the past or ever hoped to experience in the future.

In most companies and organizations an overseas assignment is a disruption of the typical career path and can even, in some cases, mean a step down upon return. Whatever the eventual outcome, an extended absence definitely means being "out of the action" for that period of time. A careful planner can, however, diminish the "out of sight, out of mind" syndrome by establishing clear channels of communication with the home office and maintaining regular correspondence once on the job. It is important to be aware of this so that you can decide whether the risks involved in such a disruption are acceptable.

If it has not already been supplied, request a copy of your company or organization's overseas employment manual to familiarize yourselves with the financial package and gauge its impact on your family finances. Important items will include housing and education allowances, cost of living allowance, tax assistance, home leaves, and possibly club memberships.

MEDICAL OR EDUCATIONAL NEEDS

If anyone in your family has a physical disability, medical problem, or learning disability which requires specialized attention, the accommodation of these needs is another important factor in your decision. Now is the time to investigate the availability of helpful resources in the destination country. For example, many international schools will refuse admission to learning-disabled children because they are unable or unwilling to provide special needs programs. Other schools may accept learning-disabled children but offer programs which are inadequate for your particular child. Medical care differs greatly from one country to another; the medical resources you take for granted in your home country may be unavailable on assignment. Facilities for the physically disabled may also be lacking. It is well worth your while to look carefully into these questions before making a decision to move. By talking with the medical department in your own organization or company and with your country's consulate abroad, you can find answers to many of your questions. You can learn from your organization or company's personnel department the extent of its willingness to assist you with any medical problems which might occur.

Some countries simply may not have what you consider to be adequate schools for your children. Or, the inherent differences in school systems with a non-American curriculum may require your children to undergo major social and academic adjustments as they move to a foreign country and then home again. Therefore, before going on assignment, you may have to weigh the relative importance of a stable and uninterrupted education versus the opportunity to live and learn in a foreign environment. You may even have to examine your feelings about "alternative" education for your children, such as tutors at home or starting your own school. While these are not realistic options for most people, they have proved quite satisfactory for some—such as the British family in Singapore who found a tutor for two of their children and the Canadians who opened a school in 1991 for the Canadian children living in Hong Kong. You may also have to consider enrolling your children at school in one country while you are in another. This can obviously put tremendous pressure on parents who are trying to decide what is best for the family's welfare. It is important not to minimize the stresses that this type of pressure can and will cause your family while on assignment. Even families with college-age children, who would be leaving home anyway, often find it difficult and anxiety-provoking to be so far away from their children. Investigate and evaluate your options as carefully as you can before making any decisions, and find out how many trips per year your company will cover for each child living apart from you.

SPOUSE'S CAREER

Two-career families often find the offer of an overseas assignment particularly stressful. While the opportunity to live in a foreign country may seem exciting and desirable, such a move cannot help disrupting a spouse's career. For some women, the move represents a welcome change or temporary

While the opportunity to live in a foreign country may seem exciting, such a move cannot help disrupting a spouse's career.

"vacation," or even an opportunity to develop a totally new career. For others, it means putting careers on hold and may pose a significant threat to professional growth. Again, careful investigation prior to making a commitment to the move will enable you to assess the degree of disruption that would result. Some wives have successfully transplanted their careers to foreign cities and even enhanced their career development. A few countries are flexible in the granting of work permits to the spouses of assignees. Unfortunately, most are not. In some countries the barriers are social rather than legal; women are simply not welcomed into the work force or are excluded from certain jobs. As a spouse, you therefore have a twofold task: you must assess the impact on your career if you leave your present job at this particular time, and you must try to determine what, if any, new career or retraining opportunities will be available to you in the new country.

Once you have gathered as much information as you can on these questions from your country's embassy or consulate in the foreign country, from the foreign country's embassy or information service in the U.S., and from local companies and organizations, the next step is to assess the implications. As with all of the issues covered in this book, there is no one correct course of action. The important thing is to be fully aware of your options and honest about your feelings concerning them. By discussing the options openly before the move, both husband and wife can avoid an uncomfortable buildup of guilt and resentment. When a couple succeeds with this type of joint planning and decision making, there is less chance of future resentment and recrimination. You will reduce the likelihood of pitched battles on foreign soil where it is difficult to deal with the accusations boiling up from inside: "*My* career means nothing to you.... You took me away from my work.... You ruined my chances." Or worse yet, from the other side: "Don't you ever do anything all day but *shop?*"

DIVORCED PARENTS

An overseas assignment poses special difficulties for the divorced parent who does not have custody of the children, or who is prohibited by a custody agreement from moving children out of the country. There is no completely satisfactory solution to this complex situation. Parents who are used to weekly visits with their children will find it very hard to give up those contacts. Most employers will subsidize one or two round-trips per year for each underage dependent, but this helps little with young children who cannot travel alone. Some will give a housing allowance which takes into consideration the extra space required for extended summer visits by your children. Finding the most satisfactory arrangement for your family may take some time and experimentation, but it is important to establish a plan for visitation and maintaining contact before you leave the country.

The other side of this dilemma is that some newly blended families find the move overseas a good opportunity to learn how to live together without the pressures and expectations of friends and family back home.

NEEDS OF YOUR EXTENDED FAMILY

In spite of the relative speed of foreign travel and the ease of long-distance communication, an overseas move still takes you far away from significant family members. Holidays, medical crises, family events, and day-to-day communication are just some of the aspects of extended family life which are affected by an overseas move. This is not to suggest that you should avoid going on assignment if you have an extended family. Rather, it is to highlight the fact that you may sense a new or intensified conflict between career and family obligations which it is helpful to assess before leaving the country. Thus, for example, a thirty-hour distance from home might seem untenable while a distance of eight hours would be quite manageable.

People who have never before lived far from the family base can find this type of move particularly stressful. For some this interruption of full participation in the life of the extended family comes as a long overdue relief, while for others it is quite difficult; and a husband and wife may have very different responses to the change. Do not minimize each other's feelings on this issue, either before you go or while you are away. You may need to support each other during times of particular loneliness, sadness, or guilt.

In your efforts to evaluate these career and family issues, a useful guideline may be "the fewer surprises the better." False expectations often lead to more problems than the issues themselves. Feel free to ask as many questions, read as many books, and make as many phone calls as you can to get the information you need. Almost without exception, people who have lived overseas will be happy to talk with you, share their experiences, and answer your questions. Ask your company or organization, church, friends, neighbors, and real estate agent for names of families who have lived overseas and *call them up*.

WHEN TO SAY NO

The considerations discussed above require your attention and may or may not lead you to question the appropriateness of a foreign assignment, but there are other family and/or personal situations that do not transport well at all. A foreign country is not a good place to mend a broken or shaky marriage, cure a severe depression or other emotional problems, or solve drug or alcohol addiction. The mystique or romance of living overseas leads people to believe (or want to believe) that everything will be better "over there" or "if we can just get away for a while." This simply is not true. While an overseas assignment can be truly wonderful and fun, it is not a vacation from life or pressure, or an escape from one's own realities. People bring with them all of their emotional baggage because it is impossible to leave behind. Problems do not get better away from home; all too frequently, they are only exacerbated. "Being away from it all" also means being away from whatever familiar support network you have created at home. Inherent in overseas living is a certain degree of isolation and loneliness which cannot help but add to problems that already exist.

Do your family and your organization or company a favor and be honest with yourselves when deciding whether an overseas assignment makes sense. Saying no now is far less painful than having to pull up stakes in the middle of the assignment and come home because it just didn't work out.

two

Breaking the News

Telling others about your decision to accept an assignment overseas can be a very complicated process. You need to be gathering as much information as possible in order to prepare for the move and yet you may, for business or other reasons, be required to keep your new assignment a secret. This can be a particularly stressful period, lasting as long as several months. Our experience has proven that having someone to talk to can help lighten the burden, preferably someone carefully chosen to help you gather the information you need. If you're lucky, this person will be a close friend who can also support you during this difficult but exciting period.

When it is time to tell your family and friends of your plans, you will find it easier if you have given careful consideration to how you will break the news and are prepared for their reactions.

TELLING YOUR CHILDREN

Parents, often out of a misplaced sense of guilt, may wonder whether they should consult their children on the decision to move. The answer is usually no. Even teenage children do not have the foresight or breadth of experience to be able to make this kind of decision. Make sure your decision and plans are clear in your minds and then tell your children.

How and when you tell the children will depend primarily on their ages. The most important thing is that they hear the news from you rather than from someone else. Therefore, tell your children your plans *before* you start discussing them with other people.

Older children usually need more time to adjust and prepare than younger children. Some will be excited and enthusiastic, eager to try something new; many will resent having their lives thrown into disorder. Whichever it is, older children tend to be dramatic and vocal in their responses. This is in no way intended to make light of the depth or intensity of their feelings but merely to alert you to the fact that they may try—and succeed—in making you feel guilty. They may accuse you of torture, cruelty, insensitivity, lack of love, and tyrannical control. Teenagers, especially those who enjoy school or have a boy- or girlfriend, may even refuse to go with you, concocting elaborate plans to remain in the home country. Emotional blackmail can be very difficult for parents, especially when you are already suffering from your own anxiety and guilt.

Generally speaking, children need and want to be with their parents, even in their later teens, when they are protesting most vociferously. They need to know that you hear and understand their feelings, that you will help them cope with what's coming, but that you are still in charge. Children have the right to be angry over unanticipated changes in their lives which they cannot control. By encouraging them to acknowledge and vent these feelings in a safe manner, you will enable your children to recover more quickly and get on with the work at hand.

In some instances it may not make sense for an older child to accompany you overseas. If your child is going into the last year of high school or facing a particular set of critical exams, is a star athlete whose college or professional career depends on team participation, or has a particular need or talent which can only be met at home, think through viable alternatives first and then discuss them with your child. Some families decide that the opportunity for an overseas experience is so valuable that all other plans should simply be put on hold for a year or two. Other families make arrangements for the child in question to live with relatives or friends (very close friends indeed!) for the remainder of high school. Whatever option you choose, trust your judgment and don't try to second-guess the decision.

Younger children are less able to comprehend the news you are giving them. They are also less able to understand and express their reactions. As a result, they seem easier to handle than the older children. You may have a calm and uneventful conversation about the move with your four-, six-, or eight-year-old, pat yourself on the back on a job well done, and hear little else about it. Please don't leave it at that.

While the younger child's reaction may be less obvious and less guilt- or anxiety-provoking, it is just as real and just as intense. You may see little connection between your announcement and subsequent behavior changes simply because the child is unaware of the connection or has a very delayed response. Continue talking with your child about the move, even if he or she does not seem interested, and be on the lookout for different types of reactions. Some reactions might include refusal to talk about the move, extra clinginess, nightmares, unusual bed-wetting, or behavioral changes in school. Some children are initially very excited about the move but become increasingly angry or sad as the implications begin to sink in or as the time for departure approaches.

It is particularly important not to minimize the feelings and fears of young children. Parents often assume that three-, four-, or five-year-olds are happy as long as they are with their parents and will therefore experience little anxiety about the move. Small children, however, have very intense personal relationships—different in form, perhaps, from those of adults, but equally meaningful. Attachments to playmates, teachers, pets, and possessions are being threatened. In discussions with your children, you may have to deal repeatedly with questions about the people they are leaving behind: "What will happen to them?" "Will I see them again?" "Will they be the same?" "Why can't they come too?" Depending on your plans for family pets and household possessions, you may have to answer the same sorts of questions about these as well.

Young children's concerns, at least initially, are usually quite specific and concrete. One seven-year-old boy was very frightened that he would have to go for two years in Japan without eating anything because the food would be so strange. Another child was worried that no one in the new country would be able to understand her, or she them. Many often worry about the long airplane trip.

Another important factor for parents to remember is that young children have a very different sense of time than adults do. They may think of time as standing still while they are gone, or be unable to comprehend the length of time the family will be away. Most young children think of the proposed move, at least initially, as a trip or vacation which will soon be finished.

Children also have very little sense of geography. If you don't already own a globe, this is a perfect time to get one. As you talk about the move, put little markers on the globe to indicate not only your new, temporary home but also the homes of friends or relatives who live in different cities or countries. In this way, your children will gradually come to understand what you are telling them. You can continue this process while overseas, adding markers for family vacations and business or professional trips.

You will hear again and again from a variety of well-meaning people that children are very resilient, that they adjust easily and love the experience. Children are resilient, but their responses to the move and to the experience as a whole will be as varied as their individual personalities and should be taken seriously. To the extent that you can be sensitive to, and accepting of, these differing responses, you will avoid a lot of difficulties.

Their responses to the move will be as varied as their individual personalities.

All children, big and small, feel more comfortable when they sense that their parents feel confident and secure. This may pose a challenge for you in the midst of your own worries and concerns, which is one major reason for being sure of your decision and your plans before talking with the children. Your feelings of enthusiasm and adventure (if you're lucky enough to still have a hold on them) will be transmitted to your children. And if you're even luckier, theirs will return to bolster you when yours are flagging.

TELLING YOUR RELATIVES

Most relatives will have very personal responses to your overseas assignment. Since you may find it difficult to deal with other people's emotions while you are coping with your own, you might do better to delay bringing the subject up until your plans are fairly well set in your own minds. If you want or need to talk over the decision with family members, you can do it most successfully with people who can be objective and supportive of your needs as well as their own.

The responses you receive from your relatives will vary greatly, from being thrilled and excited for you to resentment and anger. Perhaps the most difficult response will come from in-laws or grandparents, who are truly saddened and frightened at the thought of having their daughter and grandchildren so far from them. The man who "takes his wife and children so far away" is sometimes treated like a villain. Grandparents, particularly those who have never traveled great distances or are not able to travel, may experience the separation as a terrible loss in their lives. They may feel abandoned and unneeded. The other side of the coin, of course, is that your overseas move may provide the necessary impetus for them to brave the long trip, thus opening whole new vistas in their lives. The elderly also fear the possibility of severe illness or even death in your absence. Having informed yourselves of your organization or company's emergency-leave policy, you can reassure your parents of your ability to return in an emergency.

The disruption of the extended-family network, particularly the relationship with grandparents, may be the single greatest disadvantage of overseas life. It is important to consider this problem and its solutions right from the beginning, with all family members contributing ideas. Talk about how you can best maintain communication—letters, audiotapes, videootapes, photographs, or telephone calls. Discuss the possibility of visits. The solution for each family will necessarily be different. One grandmother, who was afraid her grandchildren would forget her, always enclosed in her family letters a personal postcard for each child.

The extended-family network will also be affected by the fact that the observance of family traditions, holidays, and major life events will necessarily be altered by your absence. As you talk about the move with your relatives before you leave the country, try to devise creative ways to share those special occasions. Try also to resolve concerns about your family commitments, such as your continued participation in the care of an elderly relative or your returning home to attend major family events. Family members may be afraid that you are abandoning them or certain shared responsibilities, and to some extent this abandonment is real, even if not intentional. It will help a great deal if family members can discuss their concerns about this openly and make plans accordingly.

It is also helpful before you move to come to some agreement with family members about "secrets." With the best of intentions, relatives at home may begin to shield you from important news about health or other problems "so that you won't worry." While you may appreciate this at the time because it saves you from worrying about things you cannot see or control, it begins to subtly change your relationship to the family, making the return home much more difficult. Family members need to be aware of these long-term effects and to realize how important it is for you to keep involved in family affairs. The form of your involvement may have to change because of the distance, but the substance does not.

TELLING YOUR FRIENDS

Friends will experience much the same range of emotions over your departure as your relatives. Most of the same guidelines apply to your discussions with them. Do not be surprised if some of your close friends seem to withdraw from you before departure. In response to feeling a bit abandoned by you, they pull back to lessen their sadness. Some people worry that your new experience will change you, thereby affecting your relationship with them. While new experiences always bring some changes in ideas and outlook, those things about you that your friends like most are unlikely to change. Only time, however, will prove this to your friends, and you will just have to be patient with them.

three

___

Learning about Your New Country

DOING YOUR RESEARCH AT HOME

Now that you have made the decision to accept a job overseas, it is time to research your new city and country and to familiarize yourselves with what lies ahead. Most companies now offer a "look-see" trip (a house-school-fact-finding mission for the employee and spouse). If, however, yours does not, you must begin the research from home. This chapter will serve as a guide in both instances. Your company or organization should provide you with a contact person in the assignment city (if not provided, be sure to ask for one). This person can help you initially by putting together a package of information:

1. A detailed map of the city with the office, schools, and colleagues' housing clearly marked

2. Copies of local newspapers, including the real estate section, which will familiarize you with local terms and give you an idea of the available types of housing

3. Literature related to living in your city—in addition to local guidebooks, extremely useful newcomers'

handbooks have been written by expatriate women's clubs or American chambers of commerce in a number of cities

4. Local magazines, weekend supplements, and videos which can also be helpful in trying to get a feel for the new country

Having made the decision to move to a foreign country, you will find that your awareness of that country is heightened. Suddenly you will notice articles (sports, business, political, and special interest features in the local papers and magazines); films, books, and conversations will unexpectedly include references to your new country. As your information base begins to grow rapidly, so will your questions. For example, political unrest in country X may never have seemed particularly relevant to you before, but now it may cause concern for your family's safety. Similarly, the status of women in country Y may never have roused your indignation. Now their social inequality will have direct consequences for your daily lives.

Seek out people who have lived in your assigned country. They are usually very willing to answer your questions and to show photos and talk about their experiences living overseas. Ask for names of people currently living in the country that you can contact on arrival. During your conversations, note the problems they have experienced. This will help you keep a balanced view, bearing in mind some of the pitfalls that may lie ahead. Remember, however, that each family's experience may differ significantly.

Other helpful sources of information include the consulate or embassy of the assignment country (as well as your own consulate or embassy there), travel agents, tourist bureaus, chambers of commerce, and school and public libraries.

Depending on the ages of your children, this information gathering can become a family project—the first step in drawing the family into the new adventure. Involving everyone in the quest will also help you identify the questions and anxieties of different family members. As you are doing your research, be alert to those aspects of the country and culture which are similar to as well as those which are different from your own. Your six-year-old may need to be told that there are toys or television in the new country, and your nine-year-old picky eater may need to know that some of the food will be recognizable. Sometimes a telephone call to the company which makes peanut butter or some other familiar and favorite food will answer that easily. Ask your local video store for travelogue tapes about your new country. This is an enjoyable way to introduce all family members to the exciting and unfamiliar sights and sounds that await you. Travel brochures lend themselves well to cut-and-paste projects for the children. Each child can make a book about the impending move and share the information with his or her teacher and classmates. Participating in this way enables children to develop a greater feeling of confidence and mastery during this unsettling period. This is also a good time to declare the adventure under way and take the family out for an introduction to Korean barbecue, Japanese tempura, or German sausage.

Another valuable and often neglected source of information is your child's school. Today more than ever before, most schools have students from many different backgrounds. Your children may already be comfortable around people who look and sound different. Some of these children may never have lived in their country of origin, but they and their families could still be a source of information on customs, foods, or climate.

Two things that no doubt weigh heavily on your minds are housing and education. It is possible to obtain a list of schools in the assignment area from your organization or corporation, the country's embassy, or publications in your library (e.g., the directory published by the International Schools Service). Find out if your company or organization has a special relationship or financial arrangement with any particular schools. Write or phone the schools to request a brochure and application forms. Once you have read the brochures, a few well-planned telephone calls will answer many of your questions, allay some of your fears, or spot potential problems. In some cities it is possible to engage a school consultant to help you assess the schools and their suitability for your children.

Try to remember that although the idea of moving to a foreign country is exciting, it is not without anxiety. It is important not to hide or ignore these feelings; encourage all family members to state their questions, doubts, or fears so that they can be dealt with honestly and realistically. This bit of advice will hold you in good stead throughout your assignment, so keep the communication lines open.

LOOK-SEE TRIP

If your company or organization offers a look-see trip, by all means take advantage of it. If not, you can use the information contained in this section to guide you in the initial week or two after you arrive abroad. The look-see trip offers a chance to solve many of the logistical problems of the move before the family relocates. In addition, it gives you an opportunity to get a sense of the city and better assess your family's ability to live there. This look-see is an expensive package for the company and deserves your full attention and hard work. It is not a second honeymoon and should not be a business trip. Nor is it the time to take the children on an exotic vacation; leave them behind. Try to set realistic goals on which you and your spouse agree.

In preparation for your look-see trip, assemble a package of the following potentially useful information:

- School records and test scores
- Medical records for any family member having special health problems
- An accurate picture of your current expenses including

schooling, housing, food, clothing, telephone, utilities, transportation, and entertainment (even though some of these will be paid for by your employer, this information will help you evaluate the overseas cost of living)
- A tape measure and rough estimate of the square footage of your present home (this will help you in choosing adequate housing and assessing furniture needs)
- A list of questions you hope to have answered by the visit

In some cases a person from your employer's local office will meet you on arrival and provide a schedule of appointments with real estate or rental agents, a relocation or orientations specialist (a person trained to guide, advise, and orient you in your new surroundings), school officials, and maybe other expatriates. This does not often happen, however, so you must be prepared to go it alone. If you have never traveled overseas before (and particularly if you travel an east-west route), the feeling of jet lag is likely to be an overwhelming surprise. By midafternoon of the first day, you will feel like you have been run over by a truck; nausea, dizziness, disorientation, muscular cramping, and strange sleep patterns are some of its delights. Try to be patient with yourselves. Take time to sit, think, and talk about what you feel and see. Do not expect to be able to get everything done in the first day or two. The following sample schedule is offered to help allay some of your anxiety. You may devise a different plan, but this will at least get you started.

Day One

Since you will not be in any shape to make major decisions on the first day, use the time for a private driving tour of the city to see the local office, different residential areas, schools, hospitals, shopping areas, recreational facilities, and areas of special interest. Take a map with you and mark as many of these locations as you can. This will help you to get your bearings and will facilitate the house-hunting phase of the trip.

Some companies will provide you with housing. If so, you can be thankful for your good fortune and do the rest of your planning with this in mind. If not, meet with real estate or rental agents as soon as possible to begin the search for a house or apartment. Included in your initial discussions with the agents should be questions about laws governing the purchase of property or procedures and customs in renting an apartment or house:

- Are rental properties usually furnished?
- Are appliances included?
- Who is responsible for maintenance and repairs?
- Is there a diplomatic clause allowing both tenant and landlord to terminate the lease with sixty days' notice?
- During your rental negotiations or after, can you be overbid by someone else?
- How much rent is expected at the beginning of the lease?
- What can you reasonably ask the landlord to do before moving in?
- How does the climate affect housing—both style and maintenance?
- Are children allowed to play in the area or on the grass outside the apartments or is it purely ornamental and off-limits?
- Are the apartments well soundproofed? If not, a ground-floor apartment may be your best bet—no neighbors below you to irritate.

At the end of the first day, you will probably feel exhausted, confused, and overwhelmed. Try not to panic and try to remember how much you liked each other before this all started. Have a quiet dinner (if you are still awake) and go to bed as close to your normal bedtime as possible. You will have plenty

of time to talk everything over when jet lag awakens you at
3:00 A.M.

Day Two

If there is more than one suitable school in the city, the
second day should be declared school visitation day so you can
determine which one will best fulfill your needs. When you
contact the schools to schedule your visit, ask them to have
ready for you an information packet with a school newspaper,
newsletter, and any other special information which will give
you a sense of the school environment.

You will probably feel exhausted, confused, and overwhelmed.

Most overseas schools have high academic standards, and
your children should be able to reenter schools at home without a great deal of academic difficulty. In addition to academ-
ics, however, there are other important factors to be consid-

ered. First, there are different types of schools providing education for expatriate children: local, overseas national, binational, and parochial schools. Depending on where you are moving, you may find any or all of these types of schools from which to choose.

Local Schools. Entering your child in the local school can give the whole family a feeling of belonging in the new community as opposed to being outsiders. Whether the local school is a viable option, however, depends on a number of variables: the child's age, the language of instruction, and the child's personality. This option is most successful if the language of instruction is the child's native language. Nevertheless, families who enroll their preschoolers in local nurseries find that their children are virtually bilingual by the time they enter the first grade. Enrolling older children in a local school must be considered very carefully. One woman, a middle-school teacher, offered the following caveat after her family's experience in France:

> Local schools are frequently much more difficult because the student is struggling simultaneously with subject matter and learning the language. Make sure your child has the capabilities (both intellectual and emotional) to deal with the stress. Many don't. In addition, one is dealing with teachers from that country who may have a different philosophy of education. For example, in France, children were sometimes encouraged to ridicule their peers who didn't perform well, based on the theory that peer pressure would goad them to do better work next time.

Overseas National Schools. Often referred to as "international schools," overseas national schools are private institutions which were founded and are run by educators of a single nationality (e.g., American, English, French) but serve students from a variety of national backgrounds. Typically these schools follow their national curriculum, teach in their own language, and maintain the atmosphere of the home country. Thus, an American child attending the American School in

Japan will find the school environment very familiar in many respects. This type of school can ease your child's transition from one country to another, though it restricts the breadth of cross-cultural experience open to the child.

Binational Schools. Both the administration and faculty of a binational school are drawn from two or more countries, and instruction may be bilingual or even trilingual. These schools offer curricula adapted from the systems of education of the countries involved, and they may offer the International Baccalaureate as well as the American high school diploma. Emphasis in binational schools is on internationalism and the appreciation and understanding of differences. This type of school can be an ideal choice for those families who believe that cultural enrichment is as important as the academic curriculum. A binational school may offer your children a wider window on the world and at the same time help them to appreciate the uniqueness of the new country in which they are living.

Parochial Schools. In many countries both Protestant and Catholic parochial schools are available. Some were started by American missionary groups and now follow an American curriculum, while others were founded by local religious groups and teach the local language and curriculum. While religious instruction may be stressed more than in nonparochial schools, admissions are rarely restricted to those of a particular faith. Because the backgrounds of expatriate families vary significantly, these schools often serve children of many nationalities and faiths. Parochial schools usually have high academic standards, making them well worth investigating. For some children, the more rigid structure and discipline of a parochial school can ease the transition into the new country.

In addition to the variation in curriculum, language, and instruction, overseas schools come in a variety of building shapes and styles, some much fancier than others. More often than not, the building style has little to do with the quality of what goes on inside. Be sure to look beyond the obvious to see what the classes, teachers, and curriculum can offer your children. As long as the building is safe, consider the architectural variations to be just one more of the many differences you will be learning to enjoy overseas.

The school your children attend in a foreign country may prove to be a much larger focus of your family's life than ever before. Therefore, you need to consider each available institution carefully before making your choice. This list should help you get started.

- Check the availability of extracurricular activities such as scouting, sports, drama, and clubs.
- Look at the library facilities. In a foreign country this may become your one source of English books.
- Ask teachers and principals about parental involvement. Many international schools place a great emphasis on the family, and most parents find themselves spending a lot of time and energy working for the school. Obviously, children in different age groups may have to attend different schools, or you may feel the need to find a particular kind of school for a child with special needs. If it is feasible, however, try to place all your children in the same school and live close by. You will find that your time together as a family is limited, and you will enjoy and benefit from the community spirit and close relationships which develop in these schools.

As you visit each school, ask to see the grade level your child is currently in as well as the one or two succeeding grades. This will give you an idea of how your child will fit in and progress. If possible, ask for names of families currently at the school and, if time permits, try to contact them. This will not only give you the opportunity to ask questions but will also guarantee a familiar face when you arrive. While touring the schools, take photos of the buildings, classrooms, play areas, library, and rooms or areas used for art, music, and physical education. This will help your children anticipate their life at a new school with fewer bogeymen. Seeing that the new school is doing units on dinosaurs or rocket ships can turn some of the fear into excitement.

While you no doubt feel under great pressure to select a school for your child during the look-see trip, this may not always be possible. For most people, the choice of school is a combination of personal preference and availability of space. Most overseas schools are private institutions, and many are becoming crowded as the number of expatriates grows annually. Therefore, placement is no longer guaranteed, even if you are applying to a school of your own nationality. Since the annual turnover in these schools is often as high as 30 percent, put your children on waiting lists and try not to panic. Be sure to inform your company or organization that school placement is a problem; it may be able to help you.

Do not be overly concerned if you are told that final acceptance of your child will be contingent upon the results of testing. This is a common practice in private schools, utilized primarily to ensure proper placement. By the same token, do not withhold pertinent information about your child's academic record or learning difficulties in hopes of easing the way into a particular school. While this may solve the immediate problem of school admission, it can only create much greater problems in the future for your family and the school.

Days Three and Four

By now, the choice of schools may have been resolved and you can focus on where you want to live (though don't be surprised if schools take up more than the one day allotted to them here). Finding a house or apartment is the next all-consuming task. Be sure to inform your real estate or rental agent of your impressions and decisions thus far; this will ensure that you see the most suitable places.

Housing may be the area of most choice and greatest compromise. Ideally, your budget and the current housing market will fit nicely, but this is not always the case. You may be shown many different types of housing, none of which exactly suits your original ideas or needs. Finding a place to live will take time, flexibility, and patience. Keep an open mind and try to remember that the fewer preconceptions or specific demands you are tied to, the easier it will be to find suitable housing.

While it may seem that duplicating what you have at home is the ideal solution to resettling a family quickly, doing so is often impossible—and sometimes the wrong choice. A house with a yard simply does not exist in many places, or, if it does, it may be a long commute from work and school, and an equal distance from other expatriate families. You may feel very isolated in a house, while an apartment can offer the feeling of safety and community support which is so vital in the early days. Remember that it is the spouse who will be spending the most time at home, who needs to feel content and comfortable, and who should therefore have a deciding vote on the housing choice.

Assess your family's most basic housing needs and communicate these to your realtor. The following factors may help you choose wisely.

Space. In countries where the climate is idyllic, limited indoor space may not be a problem. If, however, the majority of time will be spent indoors, you may need more space and will have to be creative in its use.

Neighborhood. In many countries you may have the option to live either in an area populated mostly by expatriates or in a community of locals. This is a choice requiring careful consideration for it will affect not only your day-to-day lifestyle but also the overall flavor of your overseas experience. Some families opt for the expat community which is typically more comfortable and/or luxurious and offers a more immediate sense of familiarity and belonging as well as a built-in social network. Other families choose to immerse themselves in the new culture by moving into neighborhoods far removed from other expatriates. While this type of cultural immersion requires a more lengthy adjustment process and a greater commitment to learning the language and culture, it also offers a unique opportunity to explore and enjoy a different way of life.

Location. Commuting distance to the office, shopping areas, and airports is an important factor, as is distance to school and school bus routes. How long will your children spend going to and from school, and will you be responsible for their transportation? Accessibility of playmates and sporting facilities and activities is also critical. Chauffeuring your children at home is time-consuming enough; imagine doing it in a foreign country, on strange roads, with undecipherable road signs.

Transportation. Decide whether you will be using a family car, public transportation, company car and driver, or some combination of these. You may need to be within walking distance of public transportation and local shops. The latter is particularly important in countries where daily shopping is the norm, refrigerators small, and freezers nonexistent.

Safety. As in all countries, and particularly in metropolitan areas, some neighborhoods are safer than others. Consult with someone within your company or organization about the relative safety of different areas. If you are the first or only family representing your company, ask about neighborhood safety when you visit the schools.

Utilities. Housing may vary considerably in plumbing, electrical wiring, heating, and in the source and adequacy of the water supply. Be sure to ask your realtor about all of the utilities and take nothing for granted.

Furniture. Once your housing is settled, furnishings are the next step. If the house or apartment comes furnished, make a complete list of what is there; this information will be invaluable when you begin to decide what to bring. If it is unfurnished, you need to inquire about your employer's policy on obtaining furniture. Some companies and organizations offer a choice of bringing your own possessions or renting/buying furniture on arrival; some make that choice for you. The decision will usually depend on local availability. In Tokyo, for example, there are excellent companies dealing in rental furniture; in Hong Kong, however, such companies are virtually nonexistent and employers frequently provide an allowance for purchasing furniture. If there have been other people from your organization in the country, there may be a warehouse full of household items from which to choose. In any case, it would be a good idea to measure the space in the house or apartment in which you will be living and to take photos. One's memory dims between the time of the look-see trip and the actual move. Bring with you a tape measure and the measurements of any large pieces of furniture you plan to ship. Now is the time to look at specific details—will your kitchen table fit? If not, then don't bring it! Check for storage space and built-in units—these will help you plan your shipment.

Day Five

The balance of your trip will be spent increasing your knowledge of the city. This will be easier once the initial questions of housing and schooling are resolved. In reality, these two issues are rarely finalized until the last minute, so there may be several setbacks or loose ends to be endured. Meanwhile, visit the parks in your intended neighborhood. Take photos of scenes that look similar to home as well as those of a more exotic nature. It will be reassuring for children to see a photo of McDonald's and a jungle gym in the park just like the one down the street. Visit the supermarkets and check the availability and prices of favorite items. If joining a church or synagogue is an important priority for your family, take this opportunity to look for one which suits your needs. While you are exploring the new territory, try out the public transportation and do a test run from home to the office or school.

If you are lucky enough to have time to spare, try to find one place that would be ideal for a first family outing. Having an answer the first time your children say "What are we going to do here?" will give you a real sense of control in your life.

By the end of your look-see trip, you may have had a chance to meet with colleagues and their spouses and perhaps even future neighbors or parents from the school. Questions on climate, customs, dress, food, and life-style are beginning to be answered. You are probably enjoying a feeling of accomplishment and are now going home with a sense of excitement and anticipation.

In all probability, the week of the look-see trip has not been an easy one and your emotions have run the gamut from euphoria to despondency and back; you've experienced frustration, anger, hilarity, loneliness, togetherness, and confusion. There may have been times when you felt that the two of you had none of the same goals in mind, and you have probably even thought, if not said, "There is no way I could ever live here." Some of these feelings will pass. If, at the end of this trip, you have major doubts, it is important to pinpoint the sources of your concerns. Then you need to decide if these factors are absolutely critical to your family's ability to live happily in the new country. If, after serious thought, you conclude that you could not possibly live there, sit down with someone in your employer's office and discuss the problem. However difficult and embarrassing this may be for you, your family, or the employer, it is in the employer's best interest, and your own, to make sure that you do not have serious reservations and, indeed, are keen and excited about the move. Now is the time to decide whether it is simply a matter of gathering your courage and forging ahead, or whether the foreign assignment would be a mistake and should be terminated before you go further on the wrong track.

Some of you will be heading home at the end of this week with unfinished business. It may have been one of those weeks when nothing seemed to come together: there was nothing available in the housing market, no space in the school, or your four children ended up in four different schools. Even though it will be difficult to explain some of these problems to your family, you have in no way failed. You have at least managed to familiarize yourselves with your new country and now must simply wait for some of the details to be finalized. The housing market changes everywhere in the world, and you will undoubtedly have a place to live before very long. Like almost everyone on arrival, you will probably live in a hotel or a leave flat (furnished housing temporarily vacated by a family on home leave) until everything is finalized anyway—it will just take you a little longer. Schooling is more of a concern, but the turnover is very high and the schools, understanding your predicament, will usually be quite helpful. If you are not sure which school your children will finally attend, bring all the information and photographs home for discussion and try to be positive about all of them. If your children are placed in a school that is not your first choice, keep them on the waiting list for the preferred one. Do, however, try to remain flexible; even though not your preferred choice, the first school might turn out to be fine.

On returning home from your look-see, you will be met with a myriad of questions from children, relatives, and friends. The excitement and anticipation you feel will be contagious and the photos and information you have collected will answer questions as well as calm fears. While there will be many things still to be learned about living in your new country that can only be learned from actually being there, you can now consider yourselves ready to meet the challenges that lie ahead.

COPING WITHOUT A LOOK-SEE TRIP

Those who do not have the opportunity for a look-see trip and have to do all of this at the beginning of your assignment will face an additional challenge or two. Typically, the husband is expected to start work immediately or has already been at the new job for a couple of months. In addition, if you have children, you will wonder what to do with them while you look for housing and furniture and visit the schools. If at all possible, both parents should be involved in these initial tasks; they can seem overwhelming for one person alone.

Your first priority should be to get the children involved in some kind of activity. Taking the children along on house-hunting excursions will slow the process down and will almost certainly make it much more difficult. You will feel freer to concentrate on the things you have to accomplish if you know that your children are settled. If you arrive at the end of the school year, look into available summer programs at the local schools or ask school personnel if they can recommend any activities. If nothing suitable is available, you may need to look for baby-sitters in the hotel where you are staying or in the neighborhood of your temporary housing. If your arrival coincides with the start of school, get the children enrolled before doing anything else. Once your children are settled in school or otherwise occupied, you can begin to look for housing.

four

Preparing for the Move

Once you are home from your look-see trip, your life will seem to be governed by an unending series of lists. While each family's move is unique in many ways, there are convenient checklists available to get you started. These can be acquired from moving companies or from publications devoted to the task of moving (see Recommended Readings). Also listed in the Recommended Readings are several excellent reference and children's books related to moving, though most are about domestic moves. Have a variety on hand over the next several months and make sure they are packed in your suitcases on moving day; they will be as necessary on arrival as they are now. One particularly useful publication for children is *Good-bye, House* by Banks and Evans. This helpful workbook provides a range of activities and exercises designed to enable children to say good-bye to their old home and become acquainted with the new.

THE TIMING OF YOUR MOVE

Depending on company demands, the first question to be answered is when to make the move. One of the frustrations of an overseas assignment is that the employee is often expected to be in his new job long before the family is ready or able to relocate. This difference in timing can be a matter of weeks, or even months, and should be one of the major considerations in planning the timing of your move.

Long family separations are difficult at the best of times; given the present circumstances of uncertainty and stress, the separation can seem impossible. While many parents feel it is absolutely essential to finish out the school year, it may not always be either possible or wise to do so. You are not only leaving an old home but establishing a new one. A move at the end of the school year can find you trying to establish yourselves overseas when everyone else has gone on home leave. Your children may not want to miss those exciting year-end events at school, but they rarely consider the possibility of not having a friend to play with for several weeks or months in the new neighborhood. This is extremely difficult and un-necessarily lonely. It puts extra demands on Mother to be entertainer and cheerful-always-ready-to-play-person just at the time she is most anxious and preoccupied. Arrival during the school year, even in the final few months, can give your family some immediate structure within which to build a life. There is no "best" time to relocate, but try to consider your alternatives thoroughly. If you do move over the summer holidays, it might be advisable to enroll your children in a summer school or camp in the new country for at least a few weeks. This will acquaint them with the school or neighborhood and provide them with a few playmates.

ARRANGING YOUR BUSINESS AFFAIRS IN THE HOME COUNTRY

Once the timing of your move is agreed upon, you are in the "moving mode." This can be a frenetic time. Tasks seem to pile up at an impossible rate, and you may find it difficult to keep your sense of proportion, priority, and humor. Try to proceed one step at a time, being careful to set aside some time each day for relaxation (or at least deep breathing).

There are some preliminary decisions which will determine much of what needs to be done. Will you be selling or renting your house? Do you need to set up a home for those children who will not be moving with you? Will you be taking all your possessions with you? Some of these questions will be answered by employer policy, others by personal choice. In either case, they require time and careful thought. For example, if you are free to choose what you would like to do with your present home, you may decide to keep it for use during home leaves. Or you might want to sell your house, buy a much-dreamed-of cottage, and invest the balance. More often, people choose to rent their homes and become absentee landlords. These choices and decisions will form the basis of your first set of lists. Keep in mind that one overseas assignment can stretch into two or three; try to look beyond the immediate future as you ponder these decisions.

Early in the planning of your move, make appointments to see your lawyer, accountant, and banker. Whatever your decision on housing, you will need to consult a lawyer for sales or rental agreements, or to act on your behalf after you have left the country. This is also the time to insure that your wills are up-to-date and that provisions are made in case of unforeseen emergencies. If you have never before appointed guardians for your children, by all means, do it now.

While you are overseas, most companies will appoint an accounting firm to look after your taxes. It is a good idea to meet and establish a relationship promptly with the person responsible for your account. If your employer does not provide accounting services, or does so only for the employee and not the rest of the family, then you may need to seek out and make arrangements with your own accountant. You will also want to inform your bank that you are leaving the country, that you wish to establish a line of communication and possibly a line of credit, and that you want to obtain an introduction to a bank in your overseas country. These early meetings are essential for both of you; it is as important for you as it is for your banker to know how to go about solving a problem (e.g., what happened to the mortgage payment?) before it becomes a crisis. Simple measures such as requesting that all letters be sent airmail and addressed by hand (billing computers may not hold enough characters to print your complete foreign address) can greatly facilitate your business dealings. Even with the best-laid plans, however, expect complications. One family's address in Paris had the same postal code as Corpus Christi, Texas; all of their correspondence arrived by way of Texas.

DOCUMENTS YOU WILL NEED

A move abroad means arming yourself with every conceivable document. You may feel like you are up to your neck in paperwork. It is imperative that you have copies (and in some cases the originals) of the following documents with you overseas. Before you move, collect them in a safe place and keep them with you. Do not let the movers pack them by mistake.

- **Passports and Visas:** These are essential for each member of the family. Even very young children should have their own passports while living abroad. Without separate passports family members cannot travel separately, even in cases of family crisis.
- **Work and Residence Permits (as required)**
- **Birth Certificates**
- **Certificates of Citizenship**
- **Adoption Papers**
- **Marriage Certificates**
- **Divorce and Child-Custody Papers**

- **Wills:** The originals should be left in a safe-deposit box or with a lawyer.
- **Driver's Licenses:** Renew your licenses so that they remain valid as long as possible, and ask your local motor vehicle bureau what is required to keep your licenses up-to-date while you are out of the country. Determine whether or not an international driver's license is valid or useful in the new country and apply for it if necessary.
- **Insurance Claim Records:** Write your insurance broker requesting copies of your past claim records for your cars. These will be a big help in applying for insurance coverage in the new country and may well save you a great deal of money.
- **Income Tax Records:** Since you might, at any time, need to produce or refer to your prior tax records, keep with you copies of tax forms for the previous five years.

Make a list of your important documents (and copies if necessary) to leave with your lawyer or a family member. Remember to include information on the location of your wills and insurance policies, as well as the names of institutions that are holding funds or particular information on your behalf.

OTHER IMPORTANT ITEMS

- **Children's Belongings:** Include as many of the children's belongings as possible. Children find it much easier to settle into a new home when they bring some of the old home along with them. Books, toys, stuffed animals, favorite quilts or pillows are all very helpful.
- **Medical and Dental Records:** Be sure to include dental X rays and eyeglass prescriptions as well as the generic names of all prescription drugs used by members of the family. **Note:** Most companies will require each family member to have a complete physical exam before going

on assignment. In addition, it is a good idea to make sure that everyone's dental care is up-to-date prior to departure; dental care in your new country may prove to be both unsatisfactory and exorbitantly expensive.

• **Personal and Moving Company Inventory Lists with Appropriate Insurance Documents**
• **Extra Set of Glasses or Contacts:** In some countries contacts may be problematic because of climatic conditions. Be sure to check this out well in advance.
• **A Supply of Passport-Sized Photos**
• **Subscription Magazines:** Arrange to have these sent to you. Even though they often arrive a month or two late, they will be very welcome.
• **Books, Musical Instruments, Family Games and Puzzles, Sports Equipment, and Supplies for Hobbies:** You may have more time on your hands than you are used to at home. These items can help fill long hours.
• **Shoes and Clothes:** Clothing and shoe sizes vary from country to country. Large or wide shoe sizes may be unavailable, as may tall or large clothing sizes.
• **Prescription and Nonprescription Drug Items:** During your look-see trip check on the availability and cost of drugstore items you purchase on a regular basis. If you are particularly attached to certain brands of makeup, shampoo, pain relievers, or whatever, you may want to take a supply with you.
• **Favorite Food Snacks for the Children:** Take a supply of your children's favorites, maybe even to dole out as surprises, to help you all through the initial adjustment period.

WHAT TO LEAVE AND WHAT TO TAKE

One of the more difficult and time-consuming parts of moving is deciding what to take. If you are required to move most of your belongings, the major work involves sorting out the junk in the closets, garage, and attic for disposal, and giving valuable or fragile items to friends or relatives for safe-keeping. For many assignees, however, the new home overseas will be furnished with an employer-provided lease or purchase allowance, in which case you can leave the furniture in storage.

If you have been fortunate enough to find housing during your look-see trip, you already know what is and is not provided. You have probably also been told by your employer if you have a weight or volume moving allowance (if they haven't told you, ask now to avoid a surprise moving charge later). All of this information will serve as a preliminary guideline. Try to remember that this overseas assignment is not a camping experience; it is a real part of your life that will last for one to five years, and then may be extended even longer. Therefore, in deciding what to take along, you need to ask yourselves which of your possessions make you feel most at home.

Different family members make different choices.

Different families make different choices—family pets, a special painting, a dinner service, photographs, books, a musical instrument. These are just a few examples of the things that a family might wish to have with them. Since it is often treasured mementos that give a home personality, these should probably be included. It is also recommended that you bring a good encyclopedia, a dictionary, and other reference books. Family photo albums are very important—these will help the whole family stay in touch with friends and family and maintain a feeling of continuity with the past. Whether or not you decide to take photo albums with you, do not keep them all in one place. By taking some and leaving the rest in storage or with someone else for safekeeping, you guard against the possibility of losing them all in a damaged shipment or warehouse mishap.

Some important things to consider while deciding what to take include the following:

- **Climate:** The climate of your new home is a very important factor to consider when deciding what to take. Extremely wet or dry conditions can be hard on personal possessions. Books, musical instruments, sensitive electronic equipment, and some types of furniture are particularly at risk. Try to check with families who have lived in-country for their recommendations.
- **Electricity:** Voltage and cycles vary from country to country. Sensitive electronic equipment and certain appliances (tape recorders and players, TVs, clocks, washing machines and dryers) will not work even with transformers.
- **Electrical Capacity:** In many countries, dwellings are not wired for the heavy electrical load required by large appliances. Furthermore, electricity may be very costly.

MAKING AN INVENTORY

Once you have decided where your things are going to go, it is necessary to compile inventory lists of all storage and shipment items. Each item listed should include its *replacement* value. Making an inventory is a time-consuming and arduous task that is best done as early as possible. The inventories will be needed to fill out insurance and customs forms and will also serve as a personal record of your possessions. You may be surprised to discover in a year or two that you do not remember exactly what you decided to put into storage. In addition to a written list, it is a good idea to take a series of snapshots or a videotape which shows all parts of your house and its contents. To insure valuable items properly, you may also be required to have valuations done by certified appraisers.

MOVING AND STORAGE COMPANIES

There are many variables to consider and many choices to be made in any move. Many of your questions about packing and shipping can be answered by reputable moving companies experienced in overseas moves. Prior to choosing a mover, be sure to ask for recommendations from the employer, realtors, and friends who have moved overseas. If possible, try to find a moving company with a branch operation in your assigned country. This will help to reduce confusion and increase reliability throughout the move. For those using storage facilities while on assignment, it is important to check credentials, obtain references, and view the storage premises if at all possible.

MAKING THE FINAL ARRANGEMENTS

Depending on where you are moving, your goods will take anywhere from two to ten weeks to reach your new home. Even air freight takes a week or more to clear customs and arrive at your door. Be sure to include in your suitcases games, cassette tapes and maybe a tape deck, a good first aid kit, favorite stuffed animals, and some towels to help you in the first few weeks. You will be living out of these suitcases for some time in either a hotel or leave flat and may need to be prepared for seasonal changes while you wait for your shipment to arrive. Allowing each child to select one or two favorite items for the suitcase will make it easier for them to part with the possessions going in the shipment or into storage.

Notify your overseas employer of your flight arrangements and arrival time. Ask your contact person to arrange with the hotel or real estate agent for any special equipment (e.g., baby crib) you will need immediately on arrival.

On moving day you are likely to feel as though you are caught in a cyclone. With luck your final lists will be short and your time can be given over mostly to watching the movers and saying good-bye to family and friends. A final word of caution: *check to be sure that all your documents, jewelry, and money are in your suitcases and that these are completely out of sight of the movers, preferably in a locked closet or at the neighbor's.*

five

The Early Days

On arrival in your new country you will probably move temporarily into a hotel or leave flat. There you will await your shipment and access to your new home. During the first few weeks in either place you may feel overwhelmed by the tasks ahead of you. If this is your first time in the new country and you have had no prior opportunity to look for housing or schools, you will need to refer back to Chapter 3 for hints on how to handle these tasks. There are two distinct stages involved in settling in to a new country: the initial organization of those details necessary to live comfortably and safely and the slower process of feeling at home.

HOTEL AND LEAVE-FLAT LIVING

Much of the initial organization may have to take place while you are still in temporary housing. This brings its own set of difficulties, since hotels and leave flats each have positive and negative aspects. While a hotel does everything for you from making the beds to preparing meals and doing your laundry, most families find that it becomes extremely claustrophobic and boring. No matter how good the hotel is, you may soon be eager to be settled in your own place. The degree of discomfort, however, may depend somewhat on the ages of your children and the style of the hotel. A mother of eight- and ten-year-old boys gave this description of her forty-day hotel stay:

> The move and flight were so tiring and stressful that I thoroughly enjoyed the hotel. It's nice to be pampered for a while after such a monumental chore—nice not to have to cook, nice to have clean sheets every day, chocolates on the pillow every night, and no cares in the world. For me it was a time to recharge my batteries before the equally tiring task of . . . creating a new home.

There are a few things that can be done to make hotel living with young children more pleasant. Ask the hotel to empty the bar refrigerator in at least one room so that you can restock it with juice, milk, bread, peanut butter, or other family favorites. This is a real bonus when nobody can bear the thought of room service one more time. In dealing with the boredom, you will have to be creative—it is difficult to keep children happy in a hotel environment. One family invested in a huge two-thousand-piece jigsaw puzzle, which became a group challenge. Housekeeping vacuumed around it daily for weeks, and it now hangs framed in the den as a reminder of this particular part of their assignment.

In some large cities there can be several families on assignment living in a hotel at any given time. One hotel in Hong Kong always has so many families in temporary residence that the International School sends a daily school bus to pick up the children. Many long-term friendships have begun under these unlikely circumstances, so keep your eyes open for potential playmates for your children and companions for yourselves. Don't forget to be flexible in your approach. One newcomer in London found a playgroup in a neighborhood park by following a respectable-looking woman pushing a toddler in a stroller.

A newcomer in London found a playgroup in a neighborhood park by following a respectable-looking woman pushing a toddler in a stroller.

For those living in a leave flat, the social opportunities may not be as great, but the claustrophobia is usually less of a problem. You will begin to lead a normal daily life complete with cooking, cleaning, and marketing while still trying to accomplish your settling-in chores. This might leave you exhausted, but it may still be the best solution for a family with children.

These early days are an excellent time to explore your surroundings. Locate parks, recreational facilities, walking trails, and movie theaters. Practice taking the bus or the subway; walk around the neighborhood of your new home and begin to get acquainted with the bakeries, meat markets, and grocery stores.

SETTLING-IN CHORES

Your settling-in chores will be of two basic types—those relating to entering a new country and those involved in setting up house. Upon entering a new country, you may need to register with the authorities, apply for driver's licenses, buy a car, register your family with medical and dental clinics in your area, set up bank accounts, and see to insurance coverage. It may also be necessary to arrange for your children to visit the school for placement testing and to buy uniforms or supplies. This is a good time to have calling cards printed for your family—indispensable in countries like Japan, China, South Korea, Greece, Russia, or Thailand, which use different alphabets, and quite helpful in any foreign environment. On one side give your name, address, and phone number in English (and the local language if the alphabet is different). On the other side print a map with your home clearly marked. This card will enable you as well as taxi drivers, delivery trucks, and new friends to find the way to your house.

Many questions and unforeseen problems will undoubtedly crop up during this time. Initially, the best source of help and information will probably be your employer. If, for example, you need a medical referral, have difficulty locating a municipal office, or cannot contact your landlord, call your employer. If the company does not have a policy to deal with the situation or cannot answer your question, it may be able to put you in touch with someone else who can help you. *By keeping the company or organization abreast of your problems, you are also helping it to improve its services to future expat families.*

EMERGENCY PROCEDURES

Now is also the best time to learn and practice your own emergency procedures. Find out how to call the fire department and ambulance, and post the phone numbers near all your telephones. Ask whether you can request emergency services in English or if you must use the local language. In an emergency situation you will probably forget foreign language phrases, so write the necessary phrases phonetically and post them with the emergency numbers. Locate the nearest hospital or emergency room and learn how to get there. You might even want to practice the route once or twice. In addition, find out whether the ambulance will transport you to the hospital of your choice (some will only take you to the nearest one) and whether you need to have a personal physician available to make emergency admission arrangements.

Find out if your area is subject to earthquakes, typhoons, or any other potentially dangerous natural phenomena. Familiarize yourselves with the necessary safety precautions and emergency procedures, then make sure that the whole family knows the information. Similarly, ask whether there are poisonous plants, animals, or insects in the area and locate the nearest poison control center. You may never have to deal with any of these dangers, but it will ease your mind to know you are prepared.

SETTING UP HOUSE

Once the initial chores are completed, it is time to deal with setting up house. The time required for this task depends greatly on your personality. Some like to decorate a home as quickly as possible so that they can get on with other things, while others prefer to move at a slower pace, making the transition into their new environment more gradual. Either approach is fine, but for the following reasons a target period of six to eight weeks is recommended. Some assignments are much shorter than originally anticipated, and if you spend a disproportionate amount of time and energy on the setting-up process, you will feel cheated by an early transfer—as though it were over before it really began. In addition, you will find yourselves spending a great deal of money during this period, since most companies, and some organizations, provide a moving-in allowance of some sort. The "heady" feeling associated with this process has little bearing on reality. The sooner the buying spree comes to an end, the easier it is to regain some sense of control of the financial realities in your new country.

The work involved in setting up house will depend largely on your living situation. If you have brought everything with you, or if your new home is furnished, then the major project may be choosing curtains. If you must furnish an entire home, your job is much larger. In any case, you will find yourself faced with a great many decisions all at once. While some people thrive on this sort of challenge, others agonize over each decision. It is worth remembering that while this is neither a camping experience nor an insignificant period of your life, it *is* temporary, and very few of these decorating decisions are forever. Try something new or re-create what you had before, but whatever you decide to do, don't spend an inordinate length of time fretting about it. In the end, it is more important to get on with living in your new environment.

Occasionally, a family is initiated into overseas life with a badly damaged air or sea shipment. This can be a traumatic blow that tends to color the early months of the assignment. Your primary task in the event of a damaged shipment is to deal with the insurance claim as quickly as possible, find a competent repairman, and then put the unfortunate episode behind you. Stewing over the problem will only serve to delay your adjustment to and enjoyment of your new surroundings. Sometimes unexpected benefits derive from apparent catastrophe: one woman found a good friend in the Australian Museum's restoration expert who repaired her antique furniture.

COPING WITH PHYSICAL AND EMOTIONAL UPHEAVAL

This early period is nearly always exhausting, even under the best of circumstances. At times it will seem as if every decision and every chore are major trials. If you have moved to a very different climate, your body will be struggling to adapt physically to the change, and this process can take several months. Pamper yourself a little. During this time, everyone is more susceptible to bouts of fatigue and illness. You may experience allergic reactions caused by changes in climate or pollution levels; ear, nose, and throat infections; or digestive problems. This need not mean that your new environment is dirtier than home, just that the germs are different from the ones to which you are accustomed. All of this will pass eventually; in the meantime, however, try to follow every mother's good advice: dress properly for the new climate and get plenty of rest and exercise.

This early stage is also a time of great loneliness. While husbands are thrust immediately into a network of colleagues, wives and children are tiring of each other and yearning to meet new people. You miss being able to pick up a phone to chat with family or friends, the comfort and familiarity of home. One wife described her emotions clearly:

> I remember feeling quite jealous of my husband's situation at this point. He was comfortably settled in his new office, which looked just like his New York office—same furniture, same planters—with colleagues he already knew, since most of them had been in New York at one time or another. Meanwhile, I was isolated from anything familiar.

Don't despair. Every one of the difficulties you are facing has probably been confronted and solved by many families before you, and you, too, will eventually find the solutions and get everything done. At some point during these weeks, you will suddenly realize that you are reasonably well settled in to a new job and new home, the children are enrolled in a school or summer program, and daily life is under control. You may even have been fortunate enough to find your first new friends. The early days of your overseas assignment are now behind you and you are ready for bigger and better things. Congratulations!

PART II

The Honeymoon Is Over ... Or Just Beginning

six

Culture Shock

The chores of settling in have kept you busy and preoccupied—maybe even to the point of not thinking very much about how it feels to be overseas. Typically, each family member will have his or her own distinct response to the new life situation, and each person will find that the feelings change somewhat from day to day, month to month.

Most families experience an initial "honeymoon" period, when daily life still feels like an extended vacation filled with the new and glamorous. It has been said that families spend more money (usually the company's) in their first few weeks abroad than they will ever spend again in a similar period of time. The honeymoon can last for several weeks or several months, but eventually the sheen begins to dull as the family realizes that this is not a vacation, but real life filled with the familiar, and not-so-familiar, ups and downs of daily living.

Each culture is different. While stating the obvious, this assertion contains within it an important key to success in your overseas experience. If you spend your time and energy bemoaning the differences and assume that your way of thinking or acting is superior, you will create unnecessary frustration for yourself, alienate others, and deny yourself the learning and pleasure to be derived from experiencing a new culture.

The honeymoon can last for several weeks or months, but eventually families realize this is not a vacation: "We've had fun, Mom, but it's time to go home now."

The people in your new country may act, look, and even smell different from the people at home. They may talk and move at a different pace than you are used to and even have different ideas about such basic aspects of living as work, play, family life, relationships, education, and privacy. You may be surrounded by a language you cannot understand, signs which are incomprehensible, and a variety of totally alien sights, sounds, and smells. As the honeymoon fades, this barrage of the unfamiliar begins to batter your senses.

CULTURE SHOCK: WHAT IS IT?

"Culture shock" is a name for the reaction people have to the differences which surround them in a new environment and to having all the familiar supports knocked out from under them. For most people, the inability to comprehend much of what is going on around them, the frustration of trying to simply get things done, and the sometimes overpowering ache of loneliness and homesickness are a new and uncomfortable experience that can produce such sensations as irritation, fatigue, insomnia, and even depression. Until you develop the ability to cope with the differences—by screening out some of the stimuli and by coming to a better understanding and appreciation of the rest—you may find yourself in a constant state of discontent.

The book, *The Art of Crossing Cultures* by Craig Storti (see Recommended Readings), provides a very helpful definition of the experience of culture shock as well as the steps required to overcome it. Storti relates culture shock to disappointed expectations, specifically to the discomfort you feel in a new environment when you encounter people who don't behave the way you expect them to. The reaction of many, if not most, people to these disappointed expectations is to feel threatened and uncertain how to respond. The feeling of threat causes them to withdraw, gradually building a barrier of fear, resentment, or even disgust between themselves and those they perceive to be different.

In order to overcome this automatic withdrawal, it is important to develop an awareness of the feelings that produce it. When you recognize that your feelings of discomfort are simply the result of people around you behaving in an unexpected way, the discomfort begins to dissipate. Because you feel less threatened, you feel freer to observe, to try to understand and enjoy what you are seeing. The next time you encounter a similar situation, you will feel less surprised and therefore less threatened. This is the gradual process of adjustment. To the extent that you open yourself to this process, you will increase your understanding and appreciation of the new culture—and your own as well.

Another book, *Survival Kit for Overseas Living* by L. Robert Kohls, outlines in concise form not only the causes and progressive stages of culture shock but also steps you can take to minimize its impact.

Most overseas assignees have had little prior experience being members of a minority group. While this may turn out to be one of the most valuable learning experiences of your assignment, it is initially quite daunting. You may be the object of curiosity, the target of resentment, or treated as though you are invisible. You may be welcomed as a guest or feared as an intruder. Whether people's responses to you are explicit or remarkably subtle, you will constantly be aware of being on someone else's turf—an unfamiliar and disconcerting experience for many.

This feeling will be particularly intense for women moving to strongly male-oriented cultures. Those of you who now take your equality for granted will be shocked to find how impotent you suddenly become. In some countries you will be unable to have a bank account, sign a check, dress as you choose, or even go out unescorted. Having made the decision to move to this type of culture, you will weather the experience most successfully if you remember that it is temporary and treat it as a major learning experience. You will *not* be able to change the system!

An additional source of culture shock for many families is their change of life-style—from country to city living, for example, or vice versa. This can be a difficult transition, described by some people as "feeling misplaced" or "physically out of sorts with the environment." In order to avoid feeling trapped by the new environment, it is important to view it as a short-term opportunity to try something new, to experiment. Occasionally, this type of experimentation yields surprising results. For example, people who have always chosen houses in the suburbs discover they enjoy the convenience, ease, and social interactions provided by city apartment living. Having always given their children a house and yard, they discover that the children like the apartment building with its easy access to playmates.

During the early months of the assignment, less obvious

In order to avoid feeling trapped by the new environment, it is important to view it as a short-term opportunity to try something new, to experiment.

cultural differences will gradually become apparent to you. Even the most mundane chores feel complicated and more than necessarily tedious. Driving on the "wrong" side of the street in unimaginable traffic conditions; buying strange foods in tiny, unfamiliar stores; riding on a bus without knowing when to get off; trying to communicate your needs to a salesperson or repairman who nods politely but obviously doesn't understand a word you have said; taking the kids to a foreign pediatrician—are difficult because nothing is familiar, nothing is automatic any more. Some of your most lasting and amusing memories will be of coping with these daily chores, but at the time they can be very annoying. No matter how irritating or frustrating the episode, try to find something to laugh about. Your sense of humor is probably your best line of defense. One mother in Saudi Arabia needed to find a potty seat to toilet train her son. After making several unsuccessful attempts to explain to storekeepers what she needed, she finally found a man who seemed to understand what she was saying. He nodded eagerly and disappeared into the back room. He returned moments later saying, "You want remote control?" One very satisfying aspect of your foreign assignment will be a growing sense of mastery and accomplishment as you gradually learn to cope with the unfamiliar.

COPING WITH CULTURE SHOCK

You can facilitate this coping in a number of ways. One valuable resource for understanding and dealing with the dynamics of the cross-cultural experience, as mentioned earlier, is the book *Survival Kit for Overseas Living* (see Recommended Readings). Kohls wisely suggests, "One of the best antidotes to culture shock ... is knowing as much as possible about where you are" (Kohls 69). He offers fifty questions that will help you become familiar with your new home. Once overseas, books about local history, customs, and culture are normally available in hotel bookstores and tourist offices. Keep in mind, however, that in-depth knowledge of customs and social rituals is not required or even expected. Far more important is a sincere display of interest, respect, and kindness. In many cities, you will find organizations which offer classes or excursions designed to familiarize you with the new country. For example, private clubs, the YMCA/YWCA, local universities, and women's groups often offer a wide variety of classes, lectures, and field trips, all of which will enable you to gather helpful information and meet new people at the same time.

The best way to become familiar with your new country and culture is to meet some of the people. This is more difficult in some countries than in others, depending on language, the neighborhood in which you live, the number of assignees in the office, and local feeling about foreigners. In some countries, such as France, it is incumbent on you, the newcomer, to go around and introduce yourselves to the neighbors. This may be intimidating, both because of language difficulties and your own expectations that the neighbors should call on you. One family solved this problem by waiting until Christmas, and then taking each neighbor a plate of cookies. The family was immediately invited to visit every family in the building.

An effective way to meet local people is to take language lessons. Most language teachers can speak some English and are used to interacting with foreigners. An enthusiastic teacher can become an ideal source of information and a good friend. In addition, some knowledge of the local language will make your foreign assignment far easier and more interesting. Many people shy away from language lessons because of the time and work involved; however, the results will be worth the effort. First, the more words and phrases you learn, the less strange and incompetent you feel. Second, the local people will usually appreciate your efforts to learn and speak their language, making you feel more welcome.

> But the most compelling reason to learn the language of another land is because of the symbolic significance of the act of communication. At its most fundamental, the attempt to speak with people in a foreign country is an acknowledgement of their humanity and individual worth (as it is, perforce, an indication of our own), a sign that we take them and their concerns seriously. And the gesture is as important as our degree of proficiency (Storti 90).

seven

Expatriate Life

Life as an expatriate involves its own kind of culture shock. Although it varies somewhat from one foreign country to another, for most families the expatriate life-style is far more lavish—and freer of responsibility—than any they have enjoyed at home.

Your family will very likely have a special living allowance provided by your employer to cover any increases in the cost of living you encounter in the new country. In most cases this allowance more than makes up for the cost differential. In addition, you may have household help, a car and driver, a club membership, and the opportunity to take exotic vacations. These perks of the assignment can be difficult to adjust to—and later, even more difficult to give up. The changes in life-style can blur family roles, shake up family values, and alter family goals—all of which is somewhat disruptive. You may well be wondering, "What can be so hard about luxury?" It is not the luxury but the fact that it is only temporary which causes some of the difficulty and confusion for most people. In addition, expatriate families often find that their standard of living is significantly higher than that of the local population. Consider, for example, the experience of an oil company executive living in Bangladesh or a computer company executive living in India. Many families are, at least initially, troubled by the blatant disparity and by some of the local residents' resentment of foreigners' life-style. Most people find that they gradually become somewhat desensitized to the poverty around them, seeing it as just one of a myriad of cultural differences to be experienced and appreciated. Parents and children will find this a unique opportunity to talk and learn about economic realities, quality of life, and human dignity.

While on assignment, the major costs of living for many people are paid by their employer. You may not even see the bills. Even if you are maintaining certain household expenses (e.g., mortgage, insurance, utilities) in the home country, your expenses are usually far lower than you have been used to. You may be free of financial pressure and responsibility in a way that most adults, under normal circumstances, never are. And it feels good. Your usual problems and concerns as a homeowner—the lawn, household repairs, painting and wallpapering, the garden—are now someone else's problems. When the weekend comes, you can do what you want to do instead of plowing through a long list of house-related chores. For many people this is a welcome vacation, a unique feeling of freedom.

In addition to having somewhat less responsibility, you will probably have fewer financial restraints than you did at home. To put it bluntly, you may have more money to spend. However, this newfound economic freedom has its drawbacks. The term "conspicuous consumption" takes on new meaning in an expat community where a not-so-subtle competitiveness may lead families to make unnecessary purchases and overextend themselves financially. Women, in particular, who may suddenly have a lot of unstructured time, often become perpetual shoppers at the expense of other more productive activities. There are multitudes of beautiful and unusual things to purchase, and expats naturally wish to take advantage of this unique opportunity. In many expat communities, you can find T-shirts sporting the phrases "Born to Shop" and "Shop 'til you drop." This phenomenon of expat life can be both the result and the cause of significant stress within families.

The term "conspicuous consumption" takes on new meaning in an expat community.

You can avoid much of this stress by discussing financial plans and limits openly at the beginning of your assignment. Make a conscious decision about how you want to handle your recently acquired luxury. Some families opt to treat the "extras" as a windfall, as a once-in-a-lifetime opportunity to enjoy new and different experiences. They use whatever extra money comes their way to travel as much as possible or buy things they have always wanted. Other families treat the assignment as a unique opportunity to put away money for college educations or retirement. Predictably, most families choose a middle course. While there is no one correct way to deal with the financial aspects of your move, it is important to come up with a strategy which you can agree on and which suits your family's needs and values. And remember, you *will* be going home again—often to some pretty hefty expenses (e.g., buying a house, purchasing a new car, redecorating, reconciling your income tax). Keep a list of these major expenses and make sure you maintain the necessary funds in reserve. Since foreign assignments can be unpredictable in length, either longer or shorter than anticipated, you need to be prepared to return home (and pay the piper) at any time.

Remember also that the expatriate families around you may well have differing needs, values, and amounts of money to spend. This, of course, was also true at home, but the differences are somehow more visible in a small community where everyone's financial situation is temporarily altered, and the perspectives that come from long-time habits are lost. As a result, some degree of curiosity and competitiveness emerges about other peoples' relative job ranks and overseas benefit packages. It can be upsetting to find out that someone from another company or organization is enjoying better benefits or a bigger living allowance than you are. There is no doubt that some industries are more generous than others, or that corporations can often pay more than, for example, nonprofit organizations. However, most employers make an effort to be competitive and fair, insuring that overseas employment packages generally even out over the course of the assignment. At any rate, it is in your best interest to forget about what others do or do not have. In making financial decisions for your family, try not to be unduly influenced by the decisions other families are making; they are not necessarily the best for you.

HOUSEHOLD HELP

Families who have never had household help may now have one or more staff living in or, at least, coming in each day. If you are fortunate enough to find employees who meet your family's needs, this is a truly enjoyable experience. You spend less of your time on whatever you dislike or find uninteresting and more time on activities of your own choosing. Again, this is a luxury which most American adults have not experienced.

This particular change in life-style provides the greatest benefits—and the greatest challenges—for the wives. Women who dislike housework, errands, or cooking may suddenly feel they've been liberated. They can now pursue activities inside or outside the home, spend more time with their husbands and children, or both. The challenging aspects of having household help can be equally compelling. First, the coordination of numerous employees will require good management skills. In countries such as Malaysia and Tanzania, your responsibility for the workers in your home extends to their family members as well. Inexperienced help will have to be trained; many will have no idea how to function in a Western-style home. You can save yourself a great deal of stress and unhappiness by being flexible and by keeping your sense of humor well oiled.

> A woman in Hong Kong mentioned to the new, young maid that one of her husband's suits needed to be cleaned. Upon her return later in the afternoon, she found the maid scrubbing the suit in the bathtub. The maid then asked if she should put it in the dryer.

> A man in Saudi Arabia asked the assistant cook(!) to make some toast. Quite some time later, the man went into the kitchen to check on the progress of his breakfast. The cook had placed the slice of bread flat across the top of the toaster, allowing the bread to brown along two narrow strips. Then she had moved the slice of bread over slightly to get two more browned strips. Having filled one side with toast lines, the cook had flipped the bread over to repeat this lengthy process on the other side.

There are a few important guidelines to follow when hiring household staff. Whenever possible, hire a person who comes recommended by someone you know—a colleague, neighbor, or a family that is leaving the country. When you interview the person, pay attention to your first impressions. Ask yourself whether this is someone you want to have living in your home, interacting with you and your children, taking care of your household. Think about the age of the person—whether he or she is too old or too young to be asked to do a variety of tasks. Ask the person about his or her family (many Philippine women working in Hong Kong, for example, have husbands and children living back in the Philippines), previous work history, and particular likes or dislikes with regard to household work. In all likelihood the answers will be quite guarded, but you will still be able to learn a lot about the person. Once you have decided to hire someone, it is a good idea to suggest a "review" at the end of a couple of months—an opportunity for each of you to talk about anything that might be done differently. The maid or *amah* (an Asian nanny) may never take you up on this offer, but you will feel more comfortable giving suggestions or criticisms if you have set it up this way.

Whatever country you are living in, it is important to look into the legal responsibilities of household employers. Both the local government and the government of the employee, if he or she is also a foreigner, may have a say in your employer-employee relationship. You will probably have to sign a contract which specifies your responsibilities (e.g., living conditions, salary, food allowance, sick pay, health care, and vacation time and travel) to your employee. Ask your employer, other expat families, and your prospective employee where to get the necessary information and forms.

Initially, many women are uncomfortable with the idea of having household help. You may, for example, feel awkward in the presence of someone else doing housework and want to pitch in to help the maid or leave the house so as not to feel useless. You may try to treat the maid or amah like a member of your family, only to discover that this leaves her feeling bewildered and uncomfortable. You may have difficulty learning how to ask for things to be done—a management skill which many women lack. You may also feel that having a maid or other servants is a violation of your democratic principles or is inconsistent with your opposition to class distinctions. These feelings have to be put into perspective. A "when in Rome . . ." attitude is not inappropriate here. It is more inappropriate to ignore class distinctions which exist in the society in which you are sojourning, behavior which can cause acute distress among those who work for you and can result in confusion and disruption in your household.

Women having household help for the first time may experience some guilt and anxiety over their own changing role within the family. With someone else doing many of the tasks that previously were yours, you may begin to question your usefulness and purpose. Compounding your own guilt feelings may be a perception on the part of your husband and children that you have abdicated some of your role. Be patient; as you redefine your responsibilities and contributions, so will they. It will take some time to discover ways to make satisfying use of this gift of free time. Once you have found activities which you value and enjoy, you will stop worrying about what the maid or your family members think of you and your new life-style. Maids or amahs who will be supervising and caring for your children must be shown how you want them to do this. Attitudes about discipline, safety, nurturance, feeding, toilet training—and just about every other aspect of child rearing—vary considerably from one culture to another. Therefore, it is important to be quite specific about your expectations concerning the maid's relationship with the children and not to take anything for granted. These expectations are best conveyed via example. During the initial weeks, spend time observing the maid with your children; demonstrate how you would like her to handle various types of situations.

If you have young children who will be looked after by a maid or amah, it is important that they all know who is in charge of whom. Some maids will tend to treat children like miniature-sized employers, responding to their wishes without question. Children, of course, tend to take full advantage, with possibly dangerous consequences.

A young maid in Hong Kong was left at home to look after a five-year-old and prepare dinner. Realizing that she needed to buy additional ingredients, the maid asked the child to come along to the market. When the child refused to go, the maid went to the market, leaving the five-year-old alone for over an hour. Apparently neither the child nor the maid realized that the maid was the person in charge.

Children will, for the most part, follow their parents' example in talking to the maid or amah. Chances are that you will not hear your children bossing the maid around or talking to her rudely if they have always heard you speaking politely and respectfully. Occasionally, however, you may hear your child talk to the maid in a manner that makes you cringe. At that point, if not sooner, you'll need to explain to your child the proper way to speak to an adult who lives and works in your home.

BUSINESS ENTERTAINING

Another aspect of overseas life which may feel quite alien to your family is the amount of business entertaining required by some jobs. You may find yourselves having to assume a much more formal life-style than you have been used to, as well as having a greater than usual portion of your social life occupied with business-related activities. One advantage of business entertaining is that it helps you get acquainted quickly with new people. On the other hand, it usually requires some degree of formality which precludes real relaxation; in other words, it is still part of the job. You will need to safeguard some of your time for real socializing, relaxation, and friendship.

Japan poses a unique problem related to business entertaining. In Japanese companies, men routinely gather after work at restaurants and bars to socialize and transact business. This is a complex and integral part of the Japanese work ethic which never includes wives. (Even when you entertain Japanese men in your home, they will seldom bring their wives.)

Western men working in Japanese offices may find this hard to cope with as it cuts heavily into family time and makes the working day quite long. Western women, who are not used to being excluded from their husbands' social life, will resent this enforced separation. And the entire family will probably resent the lonely evenings and Saturdays when Dad is out socializing with business associates.

All of these changes—luxuries, role changes, household help, business socializing—are prime examples of the kind of cultural adjustments your family will have to make. To minimize the disruption caused by these aspects of expat life, it is helpful to have read and thought about them ahead of time, to discuss them as a family when they occur, and to remember that they are temporary.

eight

How Is Everyone Coping?

The adjustment to an overseas move is a complex, ongoing process. For better or for worse, family members often experience their highs and lows at varying times. It is important to recognize this so that you can be supportive of one another.

HUSBANDS

Assuming again that you are the employee, you are probably working harder and traveling more than you have in the past. At the same time, you are learning to work in a different cultural setting with people of different cultural backgrounds. This can be the most exciting, challenging, and frustrating aspect of your overseas experience. The working style and pace that you have developed throughout your career may not be in sync with your new environment. The contract you had assumed would be signed within a month may still be dragging along at five months. The project you are most excited about may not only be plagued with delay after delay but may be shelved indefinitely. Patience and flexibility begin to take on a new meaning.

You may be performing a job which did not previously exist, or which is quite different from the one you were led to expect. This will require unprecedented creativity on your part. While some of you will relish this creativity and the relative inaccessibility of guidance from headquarters, others will find it irritating or overwhelming.

Professional loneliness may also be a new part of your experience. Working in a foreign office with foreign nationals may mean that you are excluded from everyday social rituals—like lunch. You may have been brought over to teach a business or professional skill to people who do not feel they need or want your help. This can be disconcerting. It will be important for you to establish one or two business and/or social contacts inside and outside the office with whom you can discuss issues and share ideas. Be prepared to swallow your pride and ask for advice and feedback when your normally effective strategies or managerial style backfires or meets with silent noncompliance. This may be the first time in your professional life that you have had to seek out this kind of support.

Time and distance are additional factors of overseas life which require major adjustments on your part. Countries that appear close to one another on a globe may in reality be many hours apart. Business travel involves frequent time changes, hours waiting in lines to leave and enter different countries, long plane rides, and great fatigue. A two-hour meeting can involve two or more days of travel. Long-distance telephone calls which once seemed so simple may now involve advance planning and annoying time differences which require you to stay up until all hours of the night to conduct your business. One wife was heard to say that if she was awakened once more in the middle of the night by a telephone cord stretched across her neck, she was changing bedrooms. The end result is that the working day seems incredibly long.

In the early months of your assignment, these problems may loom large. As you gradually adjust to the new environment and your new role takes on clearer definition, the challenge and excitement grow. Each day can bring new experi-

ences and ideas, a complex variety of business or professional problems, and opportunities to view your work from a multitude of new perspectives. Experiencing this kind of satisfaction in an overseas assignment is one of the many factors which make people reluctant to return home when their term is up.

Most assignees do, however, return home. As a result, questions about rejoining the domestic work force are common. You may be concerned about the availability of a good position in the firm or organization upon your return, or about being forgotten while you are away. You may worry about your ability to fit back into the domestic operations if the area of your expertise has been shifted elsewhere. These are realistic questions which will need some of your attention while on assignment. You have also developed a variety of new skills which may not be appreciated or put to good use when you return. It is well worth your while to maintain good contacts in your home office and keep yourself as "visible" there as possible while you are gone. Keep current with trends and changes in your professional field and in your firm or organization. Think about what you are learning, what you are interested in, and what you would like to do next—just in case someone asks.

And, just in case all this isn't challenging and time-consuming enough, try to bear in mind that your family needs just as much—if not more—of your time and attention as they had at home. While you are deeply engrossed in the foreign work assignment, your spouse and children are attempting to establish a new life for themselves. Your sensitivity to their efforts will further their success and ultimately add to your own comfort and enjoyment. Leave enough time in your busy schedule to enjoy family activities in the new culture. Long after the daily business problems have faded from memory, you will think back on the new experiences you shared as a family.

KIDS

There are three important points to remember from our earlier discussion about your children's adjustment to an overseas move: parents are not always accurate in their predictions of how each child will react; children may have delayed reactions to the upheaval in their lives; and children, especially young ones, do not have the ability to conceptualize the move temporally or geographically, or to verbalize their feelings about it.

Parents typically expect that the move will be more disruptive for older children than for younger ones, and consequently more attention is usually paid to the educational and social needs of the older children. While this may be true in some families, it is important to remember that older children may simply be more vocal about their feelings. Young children from two to five, having only minimal understanding of the overseas move, may simply be waiting quietly for things to return to normal. As time passes and "normal" is nowhere to be found, young children may become distressed. Since this distress might be delayed for weeks or even months and take on any one of a variety of forms, it may go unrecognized. Keeping storybooks about moving on hand to read periodically with your young child may help, often making it easier for the child to put some of the painful feelings or confusion into words.

As discussed earlier, take care not to minimize the importance of young children's early relationships with playmates or teachers. These early attachments from day-care or nursery school have greater meaning for children than adults realize. Parents often find that preschoolers are grieving for friends they have left behind. Photographs, letters, or tapes may be as valuable for the youngest members of the family as they are for the oldest. One mother, who has lived in several foreign countries, helped her young children maintain a sense of continuity by providing each with a large bulletin board covered with photographs of family and friends. She also made a photo-storybook of each child's life.

Young children may initially be quite frightened in a country where everyone looks and sounds different from what they are used to. During his early weeks in Tokyo, one four-year-old boy said repeatedly (in an embarrassingly loud voice) that he didn't like the Japanese. It was some time before his parents were able to elicit the following explanation: "I don't like the way they look and they don't understand me." Fortunately, this little boy attended a binational school where he met some Japanese children and began to learn their language. Another young boy moving to Tokyo at age four developed his own language, incomprehensible to both the Japanese and his parents. The language disappeared after a few weeks as the boy felt less uncomfortable in the new environment and found some Japanese people with whom he could communicate.

Many young children moving to Asia find that they are the object of blatant curiosity. Blond children, in particular, are likely to be stared at, patted, or even hugged by admiring strangers. This can be disconcerting for children and parents

alike. Reassure your children that these strangers mean them
no harm. One little girl in Korea coped with this uncomfortable situation by wearing a hat everywhere she went.

Older children, however excited they may be about moving overseas, will find the initial adjustment difficult. This is
to be expected, and any child who does it without any apparent distress is going to let loose sooner or later. Adjusting to
a new home, entering a new school (possibly with a different
curriculum and different standards), finding new friends and
leaving old ones behind—all are difficult, and children have
even less choice about these matters than their parents do.
Thus, even children who seem to be enjoying themselves immensely may experience periods of real anger. This anger is
an appropriate response to the disruption in their lives and
should not, if expressed in a reasonably acceptable fashion, be
ignored or punished. It should probably even be encouraged.
By accepting your children's feelings as real and important,
you give a strong message of love and support. This will help
as much as anything to diffuse the anger and help them get
on with life.

Older children, with their more accurate perception of
the passage of time, may resist entering into their new community because they "will only have to say good-bye all over
again." This also is a natural, if not satisfying, response to a
disruptive situation. It is understandable that children want
to protect themselves from further pain and sadness. Nevertheless, it is important to encourage their efforts to make new
friends. Children need to understand that avoiding friendships
now may indeed prevent the later pain of separation, but that
life will be pretty bleak and lonely in the interim.

Middle- and high-school-age children may have some
initial difficulty finding friends and joining a social group.
Some children who have moved frequently, or who have lived
overseas surrounded by others who move frequently, jealously
guard existing relationships. As a result, cliques may be particularly prevalent, and your children may not be welcomed
in as friendly a way as they would like. Encourage them to join

school and community activities and to be as patient as they can—friendships will come.

WIVES

Wives and mothers are discussed last for a reason: your experience is unique within the family. Assuming again that your husband is the employee, you are the only family member whose daily life does not have a ready-made structure. Household chores may be attended to by domestic help. Your husband and children are busy with work and school. You may be surprised to feel envious, even resentful, of their automatic "in" while you flounder about trying to make some sense out of your life. You have left behind the myriad of job and home responsibilities, relationships, and commitments which provided structure in your life. Some women find this sudden freedom a welcome change. One woman recalled her move to London in the following way:

> I felt a sort of relief that I had left all this behind. Moving was an easy exit from clubs, baby-sitting pools, and volunteer commitments. I liked the idea of starting over with a clean slate, to pick up and choose the things I wanted to be involved in.

Relieved or not, you must build a life-style from scratch—a formidable task, most obviously because of the unfamiliarity of the new surroundings. The options may seem at the same time frustratingly limited and frighteningly limitless. There is a large new world around you, but, at least initially, you may have almost none of the tools necessary to explore it. Your knowledge of language, transportation, geography, and local currency is sketchy at best, and you have no companion with whom to face this new world. No wonder many women simply stay at home.

In addition, you may find it difficult to establish your own individuality because other people will tend to identify you with your husband's employer. On meeting new people, you will frequently be asked, "Who are you with?" meaning, of course, "Who does your husband work for?" At home, someone meeting you for the first time might never even think to ask this question. In other words, there is more of a tendency for people to see you as your spouse's counterpart rather than as an individual with your own interests, talents, and skills. This puts an extra burden on you to assert yourself and be creative in finding ways to put your abilities and talents to work. Not only will others begin to appreciate you as a total person, but putting your creative energy to work will also help you to maintain your own confidence and self-esteem.

The company or organization may assume a much greater involvement on your part than it would at home. You may be expected to be a guide for visiting wives, a hostess for dinner parties, or a chairperson of charity events, all because of your husband's position. This identification with his employer may cause you confusion, frustration, or resentment, especially if you have been used to pursuing your own career and interests. In spite of these difficulties, you will be trying to create a life that meets your personal needs as well as those of the family and the company.

The challenge lies in getting to know your new environment well enough to identify those activities which will prove not just entertaining but also satisfying, which won't just *fill* your time overseas, but enable you to use it productively. Then when it is time to return home, you will be able to look back on the assignment and feel good about it. You will be able to identify what you have accomplished or learned and the ways in which you have grown.

Obviously, not all women will choose the same life-style. Some will opt to immerse themselves in the new culture— exploring; taking language, history, and culture classes; establishing relationships with local women; and learning native crafts. Other women find it more satisfying to keep the overseas experience as much a continuation of home life as possible, by doing volunteer work in schools and local organizations or by continuing careers, so that the transition back home seems smoother.

Your choice may well depend on the anticipated length of your overseas assignment. Many women report that they find the initial twelve to eighteen months of assignment to be a welcome and enjoyable break from normal routine. After this length of time, however, they begin to feel a need for a more goal-oriented, purposeful structure in their everyday lives. This is the time when many women begin to look for jobs or volunteer commitments which make use of their skills and are more relevant to their long-term goals.

Women who were working full-time in the home country may find the sudden increase in leisure time somewhat daunting. The initial few weeks of unstructured time feel like a vacation, but the succeeding weeks may begin to feel somewhat burdensome until satisfying uses are found for the new freedom.

Women who wish to work may find their efforts frustrated. Rarely do both husband and wife arrive overseas with jobs already arranged. Therefore, you have to job-hunt in a foreign country which may not grant you a work permit or which frowns on women in the work force. In some countries, part-time, professional work is unavailable and the full-time workweek is six days. Given these problems, you will have to be flexible and creative in your approach. While the perfect job or work situation is probably not available, good opportunities to utilize your current skills and develop new ones usually are. For example, a woman in Saudi Arabia used the time overseas to complete a correspondence course in interior design. Another woman, living in Tokyo, used her artistic skills to create attractive jewelry out of traditional Japanese paper. Some of your best leads and suggestions will come from other expat wives, so do not hesitate to ask around for help.

Women often find loneliness a particular problem overseas. This is especially true for those who have left children or grandchildren in the home country. Even women whose children are starting college and would not have been home in any case feel "just too far way." Large telephone bills are not at all unusual during the initial months.

To make matters worse, husbands may be gone on business trips much more frequently than they were at home. Depending on the country and type of overseas assignment, a husband can travel as much as 80 percent of the time. One woman commented, "I know we were married when we came over here but now I'm not so sure." Many couples find this a new and unanticipated stress on their relationship. Departures are difficult, often beginning with an emotional distancing (or huge fight) a day or two before the trip. Reunions after extended business trips can also be fraught with tension. Your husband may return feeling relaxed, relieved, and loving, only to find you tense, resentful, and preoccupied (after all, he wasn't there when you needed him). Or, he arrives jet-lagged and exhausted to find you relaxed, relieved, and loving. It is important for both of you to recognize these differences and be patient. Being honest with each other about how you feel will help reduce the risk of misunderstandings and hurt feelings. Try to set aside some time, no matter how short, to be together and talk about what each of you has been doing and thinking about during the time apart. Finding time alone may be difficult because the children need their father's attention too. So try, if possible, to divide his limited time between a family activity, relaxation time for him, and time for you as a couple. With some practice, these transition times will become easier and you may even find yourselves able to laugh about it all.

You will need to rely heavily on your own inner resources (which, incidentally, can prove to be very educational and immensely satisfying), and you will need to reach out to other women in your community. You may well find that the relationships you form with other expat wives are among the most enjoyable and important parts of your overseas experience. It is not unusual for mothers and children to share potluck suppers with other families whose fathers are away. This helps to ease the loneliness of evening hours and provides a feeling of family.

Husbands' extended business travel may also interfere with weekend social activities. Do not hesitate to accept invitations to join other couples when your husband is away. Being a "third wheel" in an expat community is neither unusual nor inappropriate. Every wife will be alone for one event or another, so it will be easy for you to reciprocate the next time around. Your alternative is to miss out on a lot of enjoyable occasions—which can only lead to a buildup of regret and resentment.

Reaching out to meet new people is easier for some women than for others; it may require a concerted effort and patience. Having school-age children helps because of the many school-related activities which involve mothers. Women moving overseas with infants or teenagers may initially find it more difficult to meet others because they have little or no contact with the school. New mothers generally remain close to home and usually want to find friends with a similar schedule. Women without children, or with no children living at home, have the advantage of immediate freedom to join classes or clubs where they might find a willing companion for sightseeing and exploration. They are also in the enviable position of being able to go along on exotic business trips.

Whatever your particular circumstance, it is helpful to become as much of a "joiner" as you can. Even if you have never enjoyed group activities or clubs before, you will find it worth your while to try one. If you don't like a particular club, try another; you will eventually find a group that fits your style. This is by far the fastest way to meet people, and it only takes one good friend to make everything look better. Locations with particularly small expatriate communities will have fewer clubs, social groups, and classes to offer, requiring you to be especially creative.

The expatriate community is a wonderful source of friendship and meaningful activities, but it is not the *only* source. There is a new culture outside the confines of that community, and it offers opportunities for learning and enrichment that cannot be duplicated at home and may not pass your way again. Take advantage of these new opportunities to the extent that you feel comfortable.

One way to gain entry into the local culture is through language classes. Your teacher may become a friend, or may help you find someone who would enjoy exchanging practice with the local language for an opportunity to speak English. Such relationships are often mutually beneficial and may lead to other friendships as well. One woman, living in Beijing, enjoyed her language exchange with a Chinese woman so much that she set up an informal English conversation class. She was repaid with invitations to her "students'" homes for dinner, and enjoyed many delightful outings she would never have attempted on her own. Another woman who moved into a totally Japanese neighborhood in Tokyo decided to teach one of her neighbors English so she would have someone to talk to.

International schools, clubs, charity organizations, nursery schools, and sports groups offer other avenues for meeting local residents with similar interests. A woman in Hong Kong who loves horseback riding became very active in an international organization called Riding for the Disabled. She was able to meet local women who shared her love of riding and eventually to establish strong friendships with them.

Take advantage of your neighborhood as well. Local meat markets, bakeries, markets, and shops are not only fun to explore but offer other windows into the culture. After several visits, shopkeepers may start to greet you, and after a few more visits may begin to take a special interest in you. The more often you go, the more comfortable you will feel. With a few phrases of the local language and a couple of small purchases, you may begin to establish friendly relationships which, though limited in scope, may be immensely satisfying. What could be better medicine for the blues than to be greeted and welcomed like an old friend by the butcher, the baker, the fruit and vegetable seller?

If you find yourself becoming increasingly isolated, staying in your apartment, or behaving in unaccustomed ways, don't be afraid to let someone know about it. Most of the expat women you see around you, no matter how busy or involved they seem, will understand your feelings. Everyone starting life in a foreign country has struggled through days of feeling lonely, overwhelmed, and out of place. Similarly, talking to a guidance counselor at your children's school or a local physician who services the expat community may help. These individuals are familiar with the experience you are having and are usually prepared to be supportive. Then, as soon as you possibly can, look around for someone who is even newer than you are. Nothing will boost your confidence, lift your spirits, or brighten your outlook faster than helping someone who knows even less than you do.

For most women who move overseas, no matter how they choose to focus their energies, the experience eventually becomes one of unique excitement, enjoyment, and opportunity. Unlike their spouses, who frequently must spend too many hours in the office to take full advantage of the new country, women have a variety of wonderful options from which to choose. The success of your experience will depend on your attitude toward it. Seen as a unique opportunity to be enjoyed, it will become one; seen as a burden foisted upon you, it can be that as well.

PART III

Ongoing Challenges

nine

Social Relationships

A family moving overseas leaves behind a large network of friends and relatives which has probably been built up over a period of many years. While doing everything possible to maintain these relationships of long standing, the family also faces the task of building up a whole new network of social relationships. For families who have lived in one place all their lives, the idea of making friendships quickly is quite alien. Rather than waiting for relationships to emerge gradually out of the fabric of everyday life, they suddenly find it necessary, or at least advisable, to pursue relationships more actively.

STRATEGIES FOR FINDING NEW FRIENDS

Setting out to find a friend is not easy for anyone, adult or child, and the suggestions which follow can apply to all members of your family. The task may require that you be more forward than ever before. Fortunately, you are probably in a community with other expats who must be just as forward as you. Usually the response you get will be favorable, especially if you reach out to other newcomers. Occasionally you will find old-timers who seem cold or remote. It sometimes happens that people who have made a good friend or two feel that they do not need, or cannot handle, any more. They have decided that in the limited time they have overseas, they are going to enjoy the few friends they have found and not waste any time looking for more. These people are not necessarily cold or unkind; they are simply emotionally full at the moment.

Unfortunately, this strategy has its pitfalls and should probably be avoided. Since families come and go, often quite unexpectedly, it is almost impossible to count on having one particular friend—adult or child—for the duration of the assignment. This is a time to cultivate as many new and interesting relationships as you can. This variety of relationships will make your assignment more rewarding and will also make it easier for you when people you have become close to have to move. Not all of your new friendships will be equally intense or intimate, of course, but there are many people around who have a lot to offer and are eager to make friends.

Some people are reluctant to form anything other than very casual relationships overseas. On a relatively short assignment and surrounded by other transient families, they have little desire to become emotionally involved. They become, instead, like long-term tourists—resisting the kinds of attachments and commitments which would make the country feel like home. Again, this is one strategy for coping with overseas life, but certainly not the one which will provide you with the most enjoyable experience. Two to three years of your life are a significant amount of time. Keeping the people around you at a distance sufficient to insure that you will not be sad to say good-bye to them will guarantee you two to three years of isolation and loneliness. Reaching out to the people around you may result in some of the most satisfying and enjoyable friendships of your life. Children will find their friendships at school, in the apartment building, and in the neighborhood. Even in a neighborhood filled with non-English-speaking families, mutual curiosity will bring children together. Unlike adults, young children find it fairly easy to engage in nonverbal activities such as tag, catch, jacks, or bicycle riding with relative strangers. Middle-schoolers and teenagers may be more reluctant to reach out to new people, but they will generally find friendships fairly quickly within the school setting.

THE APARTMENT BUILDING NETWORK

Expats living in an apartment building for the first time often develop a very special relationship with other expats in the building. Neighbors may come to be like your extended family, gathering for holiday meals, Sunday brunch, and family events. Children, in particular, benefit from this kind of substitute extended family, running in and out of each other's apartments, feeling comfortable and secure in different households. Even if your family values privacy, peace, and quiet, you may find this kind of social network within the building to be helpful and supportive at a time in your life when you need it.

ORGANIZATIONAL OR COMPANY SOCIAL LIFE

It is not unusual for families from the same company or organization to form a social group. At the beginning of your assignment, this can be a welcome source of friendship, information, and support. There are some good reasons, however, for branching out beyond your own business and professional community. Issues of rank, confidentiality, and organizational policy can sometimes interfere with a relaxed social relationship. Professional jealousies and competitiveness can place a strain on friendships, particularly in a relatively small expat community.

You will probably find it more interesting and fulfilling to have social and recreational outlets which are totally separate from your professional life. Your child's school, the local

Even if your family values privacy, peace, and quiet, you may find the social network within the apartment building to be very helpful.

athletic clubs, your church or synagogue, and international charitable organizations are all good places to meet people of different nationalities. Local people who are interested in meeting foreigners may seek you out in any one of these situations and prove invaluable as friends and guides during your stay in the country.

LOOKING BEYOND THE EXPAT COMMUNITY

As you look around for new and interesting people to meet and enjoy, you may find that "locals" in the community seem to avoid getting to know you. Although you may look like them and speak their language, as for example, in England or Australia, you are transients. One American expat in Sydney was told by a local woman, "I can't afford to get to know you—you'll just leave again." Try not to give up too easily.

Friendships with host nationals, as also discussed in Chapter 8, can provide you with a different and exciting view of both their country and your own, and such friendships often survive the assignee's departure. One woman described her family's friendship with a Japanese-American couple they met in Tokyo:

> We met our friends at the children's school. The wife had come from New York to attend graduate school in Japan and married a Japanese professor. They live a totally Japanese life—but with an American sense of humor. They became our very close friends and the best possible guides to our new country. We were taken to out-of-the-way places which we would never have discovered by ourselves. We were shown the sights through Japanese eyes. Best of all, the friendship survived our move to Hong Kong and then back to the United States. Now we meet yearly on Cape Cod and between visits run up large phone bills.

ten
―――

Parenting Overseas

Parenting is an exciting job no matter where we do it. There are aspects of expat life, however, which can make the job particularly confusing and which impose on parents some special responsibilities.

MAINTAINING FAMILY VALUES

Children, as well as their parents, are suddenly exposed to a life-style abroad which is different from the one back home. A fancier house, private school, live-in maid, driver, and exotic vacations are new experiences for most children and may quickly begin to be taken for granted. This is especially true for very young children, for whom the assignment represents a significant proportion of their early childhood. They begin to believe that life has always been, and will always be, just like this.

Under these circumstances parents easily become concerned about their children's sense of responsibility and the values they are developing, particularly when the children begin to feel either entitled to the luxury or, worse yet, deprived because someone else has even more. Examples of attitudes which are troublesome to some parents might include the following:

- A teenager is overheard complaining to her friend that she can't go skiing in the Alps this Christmas because her parents are forcing her to go to Thailand.
- A child has trouble understanding why he needs to pick his clothes up off the floor, make his bed, or clear his plate, because "the maid will do it."
- Two four-year-old boys coming home together to play had the following conversation in the car:

  Matt: "Is your sister home?"
  Edwin: "No, she comes home from school later."
  Matt: "Is the maid home?"
  Edwin: "We don't have a maid."
  Matt: "Then who's going to open the door?"
  Mom: "Don't worry. I can open the door for us. We'll be just fine."

- A teenager in Hong Kong (the "shopper's paradise" of the world) announced she could not buy new clothes there because the "cool" stuff was only available in the U.S.
- A seven-year-old boy remarked after hearing that the plane reservations had been bungled, "They expect us to fly all the way to Paris *in coach*?!?"

Parents who are aware of and anticipate these issues related to family values and responsibility will be somewhat prepared the first time one of their children says something which makes their hair stand on end. Although families obviously differ in their values, rules, and expectations, some general guidelines may be useful.

- Be very clear with your children about your own values and priorities. This will also help you in case the perks of expat life are getting to you too.

- Remind your children periodically that your overseas assignment is temporary, unique, and a very special experience.
- Make sure that each of your children continues to have responsibilities around the household. This may even involve a few "make-work" tasks for younger children. Even if you have enough household help to do all the work, you do not want to deny your child the feelings of importance and accomplishment which come from contributing to the family welfare.
- Help your older children understand that there will always be other children or families who have more than you do—that is a fact of life. Encourage them to be happy enjoying the things they do have instead of complaining about what is missing. In addition, it is helpful to include children in some of the choices you make about purchases, vacations, and family activities so that they can appreciate the fact that choices *are* made—that no family can have and do everything.
- As you visit different cities and countries, help your children see that most of the world lives very differently from the way they do. This is not designed to make them feel guilty or uncomfortable but simply to provide a clearer perspective on how much bigger and more varied the world is than their own community.

ESTABLISHING FAMILY RULES

Family rules are important regardless of the country you are in, but expat families may find this issue particularly worrisome, especially for older children. Three factors seem to cause problems: greater personal safety in some cities (e.g., Tokyo and Hong Kong), easy access to drugs and alcohol, and limited availability of structured activities for teens. Tokyo provides a very good example of the problems facing the parents of teenagers. One of its prime attractions as a residential city is its relatively safe streets, day or night. Even your ten-year-old can ride the subways and buses and walk in safety. On the other hand, beer, liquor, and condoms are sold in corner vending machines with no apparent restrictions. Many bars and nightclubs do not observe any age requirements. Parents find themselves in somewhat of a quandary when trying to establish reasonable and enforceable rules for their children. Many in Tokyo have expressed great relief that high school students are not permitted to get driver's licenses, which at least eliminates worries about drunk driving. Japanese children, of course, live under cultural and parental restraints which defuse the problems engendered in children from more permissive cultures.

Most children, whether living at home or overseas, will put pressure on their parents to give them more freedom. "But *everyone* is doing it" is a familiar refrain. Most parents can deal with this kind of pressure reasonably successfully, as they would at home. The difference is that parents occasionally let guilt over their children's unhappiness at being taken abroad and anxiety over their children's adjustment cloud their judgment. The following suggestions may help:

- When you arrive in the new community, spend time with your child researching available activities, programs, or clubs for the appropriate age group. Look into school-sponsored sports and activities, and if none exist, try to start some.
- Encourage your children to bring friends home, and if possible, meet their parents. You will know very quickly whether you feel comfortable with the company your child is keeping.
- Make your home available for get-togethers and then *be there* to oversee things. Children need safe and comfortable places to socialize, and if they are at your house, you know where they are and whom they are with. Many parents become so involved in their own social

lives or travel that they relinquish too much control. One live-in maid cannot, and should not, be expected to supervise a group of teenagers.

• Talk to other parents to find out what is available for children, what their children are doing, and what their family rules are. Chances are you will find that everyone is *not* "doing it," and at the same time you will be educating yourselves about the social environment for teens.

• Have family discussions (as often as necessary) to establish and reinforce reasonable and acceptable rules. State your expectations explicitly and be as consistent as you can. At the same time, listen carefully to your children. Their need to make friends, be accepted, and fit in will necessarily color their judgment somewhat. You can respond in a supportive way to their feelings and offer assistance without giving in to requests you consider unreasonable, unsafe, or inappropriate.

BEING A SINGLE PARENT WHEN YOU ARE NOT ONE

Because of the heavy work and travel schedules of many men overseas, mothers find themselves in the baffling position of having to function like single parents even though they are not. One woman in England described the problem this way:

> There are many loving, wonderful husbands . . . they are just not here, and if they're not *here*, it doesn't much matter if they're in Rome, Singapore, or Baltimore. When a woman finds she can handle the situation, however, it's a great boost for her self-confidence.

There are two problems associated with this peculiar, single parent role.

Parental Teamwork Runs Amok

As their children grow, parents typically develop a pattern of teamwork which involves different duties and activities for each parent. For example, the father might assume greater responsibility for discipline, sports activities, Boy Scouts, and outdoor activities, while the mother is more the nurturer, meeting everyday needs and helping with homework and chauffeuring. Whatever the usual division of labor is, all family members come to recognize it. Typically, however, the family dynamic and living style change somewhat when the father is away for long periods. The mother needs, and wants, to fill the gaps left by his absence, making an increasing number of unilateral decisions, meting out more of the discipline, and handling a lot of the "father activities." Day-to-day life may become less formal while Dad is away, and different rules may be emphasized or enforced. Whatever changes occur, the more prolonged his absence, the more apparent is the difference when he returns.

The father comes home after an extended time away expecting the household, and his role in it, to be unchanged from the last time he was home. Instead, he sometimes feels like an intruder in an unfamiliar routine. The mother, who has grown accustomed to being in total charge, may resent interference. She may have weathered the strain of learning how to "father" and find it difficult or awkward to relinquish her new role. She may have gotten used to the more relaxed routine and bridle at having to march to the beat of the "other" drummer. In other words, the parents are no longer functioning like a team.

While some changes in the family system are inevitable when one parent is absent for extended periods, there are positive steps you can take to minimize the resulting stress. Be alert to changes in your household and your parenting roles as they occur and *talk about them*, being honest with each other about how the changes feel—good or bad. It is particularly important for fathers to realize that the family life-style and routine do not remain static while he is away, but adapt to accommodate his absence.

Acknowledge the pressures and be sensitive to each other's needs. A wife who has to take on a more comprehensive, authoritative position in the family needs her husband's emotional support to make it work. If this support is lacking, family members become confused and polarized. Children begin to feel divided in their loyalties, or family life is simply "put on hold" until Dad comes home. Conversely, a man who must be absent from home a great deal continues to think and feel like a father even while he is away. His wife should make every effort not to exclude him from this role when he returns, even though she has become accustomed to coping alone.

Another way to minimize stress is to work at maintaining consistency and agreement in your dealings with the children. This will prevent them from being able to play one of you off against the other. Discipline cannot await the arrival of a traveling father, so be sure to discuss disciplinary questions, problems, and strategies while you are together. Mom can then handle discipline problems when they occur, without risk of being second-guessed when Father returns.

Finally, try to keep in close touch by telephone during extended business trips. Fathers who are able to stay abreast of "current events" at home have a much easier time moving in and out of the family circle. A father's ongoing participation in family decisions insures that his opinion will continue to be counted and valued. In addition, his ability to keep up with school events, homework projects, and daily crises will reduce the need for him to become reacquainted after each absence.

Mom Takes the Blame

Children may become very angry at a father who is absent for prolonged periods of time. Because their time with him is so limited, however, they tend to direct their anger elsewhere—anywhere, in fact, except at him. Sometimes they direct the anger inward, at themselves, taking personal blame for his absences. "There must be something wrong with me, otherwise he would love me enough to stay home more" is a fairly common feeling among children. Sometimes the anger shows itself in behavior problems at school or with friends. More often, though, children vent their anger at the parent who is with them most of the time—Mom. The result of this is twofold: first, Mom has the double task of handling her own feelings of loneliness, loss, and resentment while bearing the brunt of her children's feelings; second, she feels caught between her husband and her children. She may either find herself constantly having to defend and explain Dad's absences (because the children hesitate to question him directly) or she begins to collude with the children in their anger at him, pushing him further and further out of the family system.

If you find yourselves on a foreign assignment requiring much more than the usual amount of business travel, the following suggestions will probably prove useful.

- Dad should talk directly to the children about his schedule and travel plans so that Mom doesn't always have to be the "bearer of bad news." Even very young children value some description of what their father is doing when he is away from home. Encourage the children to share their feelings with both of you; you, in turn, can share your feelings about the changes in life-style. This will reduce the buildup of resentment and help prevent family members from taking sides.
- Mom should speak up if she starts to feel she is fielding too much of the children's anger. Children need to understand that they have a right to their feelings, that they can talk about them with both their parents, but that they cannot beat Mom over the head with them.
- While away, Dad should communicate as frequently as possible with the children. Postcards are great. One seven-year-old American in England shared with her class her father's postcards from U.S. cities, which led to a special project on American geography. Frequent

communication will lessen the children's anger at their father as well as their need to put him on a pedestal when he returns home. They will then feel freer to share all their feelings with him—negative as well as positive.

• Dad should tape himself reading a few of the young children's favorite bedtime stories. This is comforting to the children and a wonderful way to keep him involved in important family rituals.

MAINTAINING STABILITY IN THE MIDST OF INSTABILITY

Overseas life is always characterized to some degree by instability—when will it begin, when will it end, where will we go next, and so on. Children (and adults) need some sense of order and continuity to provide an inner security even when external factors are in flux. There are many ways in which parents can promote the sense of order and continuity.

Although your life overseas may differ in many respects from life at home, it is still possible to maintain stable family routines. Young children in particular thrive on routine: household chores, weekend outings, going to church or synagogue. It does not matter what you choose, each family's needs will be different. What does matter is that you have some predictable routines in your daily life.

If religion has provided an important emotional, philosophical, or social focus for your family in the past, you will probably want to find a place of worship in your new community. Depending on your country of assignment, you may not be able to find exactly what you are looking for. However, if you are willing to be flexible you will probably be able to find others who share somewhat similar beliefs and enjoy a sense of religious community. If you cannot find a suitable place of worship in the neighborhood, you might consider taking advantage of your time overseas to learn about different relig-

Frequent communication will lessen the children's anger at Dad as well as their need to put him on a pedestal when he returns home.

ions, or you could seek out others like yourselves who would enjoy starting a Bible study class at home.

Although it can take a great deal of time and effort on your part, helping your children maintain important relationships in your home country will prove well worth your while. Exchanges of telephone calls, photos, letters, audiotapes, or videotapes will help your children remember friends and relatives while at the same time enabling those at home to watch your children grow. Home leave also provides the opportunity to spend time with some of these important people, giving children a feeling of continuity that will later smooth the transition back home.

Maintaining family holidays and traditions also promotes the feeling of stability. While part of the fun and joy of living in a foreign country is learning new traditions and customs, it is important to keep up the old. Use familiar decorations, cook traditional foods, and gather with neighbors to share the holidays. This is an important part of home which you can carry with you wherever you go, and you can add to your enjoyment by sharing some of your family's traditions with local families.

The responsibilities and challenges of parenting overseas may sometimes feel overwhelming. Through it all, however, we have the opportunity to watch our children grow in unique ways. As they adapt to a new culture and experience the unexpected, their worldview is broadened. They develop an understanding of and appreciation for differences between people and learn to view their own country and culture from a new perspective. Children develop a sense of themselves and the world that is truly special. They gain confidence in their ability to handle new and unfamiliar experiences while learning how to feel at home in a variety of environments. Having lived in and visited different parts of the world, children begin to care about the history, culture, and current events of those places. They seek out news stories, movies, and books about the countries they have seen; they feel a part of the places they have been and the places become a part of them.

eleven

Making the Most of Home Leave

THE PURPOSE OF HOME LEAVE

Fortunately, most corporations and organizations include home leaves in the assignment package, and their purpose for doing so is usually multifold:

- To allow the employee and his family time to transact family business (medical, dental, legal, and financial)
- To enable the employee time to be with other family members
- To provide time to shop for those items not readily available in the assigned country
- To guarantee the employee a few days in the home office so that he can reconnect with colleagues and feel connected to current policies and changes
- To allow time for a family vacation

As desirable as home leave is, however, it is not without its challenges and frustrations. Most of the problems seem to stem from trying to accomplish all of the above objectives, then returning overseas exhausted, unfulfilled, and in need of a holiday. Although everyone approaches home leave with different feelings and expectations, most families start out trying to please everyone—the employer, relatives and friends, and themselves. Given time and budget constraints, this is virtually impossible; nevertheless, almost all families try it at least once. The result is often a feeling of being pulled in too many directions, saying hello and good-bye an endless number of times, and pleasing almost no one.

Most families start out trying to please everyone. The result is often a feeling of being pulled in "too many directions."

While the logistics of home leave are complicated, the benefits are well worth the effort. You have the opportunity to touch base with the home front and catch up with everything from real estate prices to teenage fashions. You reaffirm ties with family and friends, albeit in a somewhat hurried and disjointed way. Your children get reacquainted with grandparents and cousins and feel part of the extended family again. So when home leave begins to seem like a giant hurdle to be overcome, try to smile, relax, and think about its positive aspects. Whatever plans you make, remember that you have given it your best shot. Don't spend a lot of time feeling guilty or second-guessing yourselves. You may not accomplish everything (you didn't really need those boxes of macaroni and cheese anyway), but with some careful planning and general cooperation, you will succeed in seeing those who are most important to you. A family reunion while you are in town can do the job beautifully. Since you have traveled all the way back to your home country, feel free to ask relatives and friends to travel the rest of the way to see you.

There may be times during your assignment when taking home leave at home seems either inappropriate or unnecessary. You may prefer to use the free airline tickets to travel to another country, a common practice but one not permitted by all employers. Be sure to check your company's policy on home leaves. Some state quite clearly that the leave must be taken in the home country and include a visit to the home office.

WHEN TO GO

The majority of organizations and companies offer home leave annually, to be taken at the discretion of the assignee. For those with school-age children, the obvious or only time is during school holidays—usually the long summer break. For those not tied down to the school calendar, there may be other, preferred choices—in time for a regular family reunion or during a favorite season of the year. In some countries, the climate may be a determining factor in planning home leave: the rainy season in Malaysia or the August heat in Tokyo.

Whatever schedule you choose, your trip will require much advance planning. One of the frustrations is the long lead time required to get travel bookings. In some cities it is necessary to reserve home-leave tickets six months in advance. This, in itself, is a cause of anxiety.

HOW LONG TO STAY

The length of the home leave is another important factor to be considered. While most assignees have a stipulated number of vacation days, the other members of the family can, and often do, choose to stay longer. Some wives pack up the day that school is out and don't return until the end of the summer. Others find the separation from husband and father too long and limit their leave to his vacation time. Your decision may ultimately depend on where you and your children feel most comfortable. Some families live from one home leave to the next, awaiting each opportunity to get back to their *real* home. Other families feel that home is the place where the immediate family lives, works, and plays together, no matter where that happens to be. These families tend to plan home leaves in the same way they have always planned vacations—as trips of limited duration to be taken when the whole family is free to go together. Ultimately your plans will probably depend on several factors:

- Your feelings about the new country and the availability of interesting activities there
- The things you want and need to do in the home country
- The availability of places to stay in the home country
- Your husband's work schedule
- What you want your children to be doing during their holidays
- Financial considerations

Whichever alternative you choose, it is wise to go for at least two weeks; otherwise, the jet-lag adjustment at both ends may negate the value of the trip.

WHERE TO STAY

Deciding where to stay on home leave is a major issue and often determines the length of the trip. Very few expat families have access to their own houses or apartments, but those who do, have two distinct advantages. First, they are able to maintain a feeling of continuity and rootedness by returning yearly to their own neighborhood. Second, they have a base from which to operate. The family can relax in one place and invite relatives and friends there for a visit. This avoids a frenetic travel schedule and the stress of suitcase living.

Most families, however, have sold their homes or have tenants in residence. Their choice, then, is usually between a hotel or series of hotels (which is usually far too expensive but does allow real freedom of movement) or staying with family and friends. Some of the strain of home leave comes from the restrictions and tensions of being a guest for such a long time. An extended stay with anyone can pale with time; no matter how welcome you were at the start, you and your hosts may eventually begin to get irritable or restless.

Obviously, visiting from place to place reduces the problem somewhat, but keeping a family continually on the move is disrupting and simply not a very comfortable or relaxing solution. Besides, your children's houseguest manners will begin to fray—or unravel—from the strain. One highly practical and satisfactory answer to the home-leave dilemma is to rent a centrally located, furnished home or condominium for the duration of your stay. The cost is lower than for hotel/restaurant living, and you can invite people to visit you.

Be sure to determine what activities are available for your children in the various locations. Home leave can feel very long for kids who have nothing "child-oriented" to do. Find out, for example, whether the school, churches, clubs, or local communities run day-camp or recreational programs. Some families offer their children a chance to attend summer camp in the home country. This can work quite well for older children. It allows them to feel part of their own country for a while—to *be* American, Canadian, Dutch, or whatever. At the end of the camp period, the family meets to spend time together with other family members and friends.

PREPARING THE CHILDREN

Home leave can be a frustrating time for children, particularly if it is a relatively short trip designed to see extended family and accomplish a variety of chores. There may be insufficient time for lengthy visits with their friends, or those friends may be otherwise occupied with summer activities of their own. Once you have decided on the general schedule of your home leave, be sure to tell the children what you have in mind. By letting them know ahead of time what they can reasonably expect, you will help them feel more prepared.

FAMILY VACATION TIME

To cope with the feeling, accurate or not, that you have been cheated out of a much-needed vacation by a round of exhausting chores and family visits, leave a few days at the end just for yourselves. One family always schedules a few days in Hawaii on their return to the Far East, strictly for R and R. Or, plan a vacation separate from home leave, which will enable your family to be together without the business and social obligations involved in a visit to the home country. Often, the knowledge of the "other holiday" will relieve some of the pressure of home leave and make it that much more enjoyable.

COPING WITHOUT A HOME LEAVE

Some people assigned overseas are, for various reasons, not entitled to or able to take home leave. For the duration of the assignment, these families have no opportunity to visit with relatives and friends at home. This can be particularly difficult for children and their grandparents, since two or three years in either's life can feel like a lifetime. You will have to work even harder at maintaining contact with your extended family. Some families have even saved enough airline mileage credits to be able to afford a trip home at their own expense or to bring relatives overseas, but if this is not an option, you will need to make do with extra phone calls, snapshots, and letters. Maintaining a positive outlook may prove difficult, especially when the people around you are talking about their leave plans. Knowing that your employer controls whether you can or cannot see your family often leads to growing resentment which colors the rest of the overseas experience. There is no completely satisfactory solution to this problem. Eventually, corporations, organizations, and government agencies will come to realize that employees will be more successful and productive knowing that they have an option to visit home while abroad. Your own strategy, in the meantime, should probably be to plan enjoyable vacations for your immediate family, perhaps at a convenient midpoint location where relatives or friends can meet you.

If you will be away from home for several years without home leave, be careful to maintain close contact with the individuals looking after your affairs. Even close friends and neighbors may tire of the responsibility after a while and request a change.

PART IV

The End of Assignment

twelve

Moving On ... Moving Home

MOVING ON TO A NEW ASSIGNMENT

The end of your foreign assignment in a particular country usually involves a lead-in of at least a few months. If you are moving on to another assignment in a new country, you can begin your preparations by applying your newly acquired expertise on overseas life. The opportunity to live in more than one foreign country and to compare different peoples, cultures, and life-styles is a unique and exciting experience and a tremendous amount of fun. The negative aspect of back-to-back overseas assignments is some painful emotional adjustment—yours and other people's—to your extended absence from home. First, "home" seems to recede further from your day-to-day experiences. You begin to wonder if you'll ever get back, and you start to question where home really is. Second, the family and friends who were expecting you back may feel abandoned and resentful, doubting whether you are ever going to return to them.

Sometimes the end of the foreign assignment comes quite unexpectedly. Some families, for example, have been told while on home leave that they are being transferred back home or to a new country. Their goods are shipped off for them and the family has no opportunity to say good-bye to friends, neighbors, business associates, or teachers. This type of departure is traumatic for the whole family and should be avoided if at all possible. Adults and children need the opportunity to plan and prepare for the emotional and physical separations and for the changes which occur in a move.

If this type of unanticipated transfer happens to your family, there may be little you can do to provide yourselves with the needed closure. Certainly you should request that the employer allow you and your children to return overseas to say your good-byes. If this is not granted, you may want to consider the possibility of financing the trip yourself—now, or as an upcoming vacation. Obviously, that would be quite expensive and may not be possible. Good-bye telephone calls, videotapes, or letters may have to suffice. Whatever method you choose, you will need to allow yourselves time to reminisce and grieve. Most people are not well suited to this type of departure, and it is to be hoped that *all* companies, organizations, and agencies will soon come to realize it.

MOVING HOME

Returning to your home country is a challenge—for some families the biggest challenge of the entire assignment. Some families do not feel ready to give up overseas life and do not want the adventure to be over. Others return to their home country expecting it to be as familiar, predictable, comfortable, and wonderful as the nostalgic picture they have carried in their minds for several years. Most find, however, that the initial months at home are disappointing, exhausting, and difficult, a kind of reverse culture shock. You may feel let down, depressed, overwhelmed, isolated, or just out of place. Like the initial phase of any move, this too will pass. Until it does, however, you must make the same efforts to familiarize yourselves with the new environment (home) that you made on arrival overseas. If at all possible, take some time on your way home for a family vacation. Particularly if you are moving back from the other side of the world, vacationing midway will reduce the impact of jet lag and leave you feeling more refreshed to face the stresses that await you. This relaxed family time will also give you the opportunity to reminisce about your experiences and share your feelings about the return home.

Moving back to your old city, house, and neighborhood makes the return easy in some respects and difficult in others. Returning to the familiar means you know what to expect, where you will put things, and how to proceed. For some families this knowledge is a welcome comfort; they look forward to settling back into the remembered routine, renewing old ties, resuming the previous life-style. For other families, returning to the familiar presents a problem. They remember their life-style before going overseas, but that style no longer seems interesting or appealing. They now prefer apartment to house, or city to suburb, or dressy to casual. Whatever it is, they have experimented briefly with a different life-style and find it more to their liking.

Some families may be going back to their home country but to a new city. Moving to an unfamiliar region of your home country may mean encountering almost as many cultural differences as you found overseas and experiencing a similar kind of culture shock, this time complicated by the fact that you aren't as prepared for things to feel strange and be unpredictable. There's no living allowance, orientation tour, or newcomer's group to smooth the way. Like any domestic move, you do it on our own with very little guidance or support from your employer. Treat this move like a new foreign assignment and approach it unhampered by prior expectations or memories. This enables you to take your time, explore the community, and restyle your new life the way you want it to be.

Whether settling in a former home or a new location, your family is once again in a situation in which it is important to make the best use of your available options. For example, if you know you have to return to a particular job, neighborhood, and house, make some other changes which reflect your new interests and tastes. Pursue hobbies you have learned overseas, cook new foods for your friends, change your household decor. Look for ways to integrate the new with the old, the foreign with the familiar. You will probably find that you value aspects of each of the past periods of your life. Regardless of the house, town, or country you are in, you can create a life-style for yourselves which combines many of these.

Returning home has been described as a return to reality, and sometimes the road is pretty bumpy and unpredictable, requiring some major adjustment. The first jolt is having simultaneously to give up a comparatively lavish expat life-style and reshoulder those responsibilities shed during the assignment. This can be traumatic, especially if not anticipated or planned for. Adults on assignment with large corporations or international organizations experience a freedom from many of the pressures and responsibilities which generally characterize their lives at home. As said before, living allowances, company-leased residences, and household help contribute to a carefree way of life. The return home involves a series of major and minor financial obligations which will be frightening and overwhelming for families who are unprepared. Buying a new house or perhaps redecorating after the tenants leave the old house, buying new cars, replacing appliances which did not survive your absence, reconciling income taxes—these are major chores involving major expenses and requiring immediate attention. Facing these responsibilities on your own, without employer assistance, may resurrect many of the anxieties you experienced as young adults leaving home for the first time. You may initially be somewhat depressed until you have had sufficient time to restabilize your finances and regain a satisfying sense of independence.

A second major challenge of the return home is the reestablishment of social relationships. Some families will be ready to jump right into their lives back home, seeking out old friends and making new ones, while others will need a bit more time. One woman returning to the United States described herself as a "voluntary hermit" for the first four months.

> I immersed myself in creating a home. I had an incredible nesting instinct. I was a driven woman, looking at, selecting, hanging wallpaper . . . and curtains. Making the place *feel* like home was my whole raison d'être. I had numerous opportunities to make new friends . . . but I think I was still missing the old ones so much that I just wasn't ready to reach out yet. Quite by coincidence (or divine intervention), a job fell into my lap four months after our return. Thank goodness, or we would no doubt have mauve, floral walls in the *garage* by now.

Most people, even if they ask about your experiences, do not really want to hear very much.

As you renew old friendships and develop new ones, you will be bursting with stories, anecdotes, and memories of your overseas experience which you want to share. Most people, however, even if they ask you about your experiences, do not really want to hear more than a brief summary. After a sentence or two, they've had enough and are ready to move on to another topic. Even in general conversation, your references to foreign ideas, cultures, or peoples may be thought of as snobbish efforts on your part to show off. One family returning from overseas made the following comment:

> We grew resentful of having to pretend that three or four years of our lives simply did not exist. Were you to tell about a vacation to Yellowstone National Park, everyone would listen. If the vacation happened to be in Spain, suddenly you become a name-dropper or braggart.

For the most part, you will learn to share your memories with each other and with other families who have lived overseas and keep most of your stories and ideas to yourselves.

A third, somewhat more subtle challenge involves integrating what you have gained from your overseas cultural experience into your life back home. No matter what country you have lived in, there will be some aspects of the life and culture there which will become part of you and part of your life-style. The friends back home may have difficulty understanding or accepting these changes in your way of doing things. One woman commented:

> While living in Japan, I became used to the quiet and cleanliness of the Japanese home. No one would ever wear shoes indoors, with the result that you never saw muddy footprints on the floor or heard the thudding of heavy shoes running through the house. When I came back to the United States, I was surprised to find that I felt a little bit resentful when visitors wore shoes in my house. I didn't want to make anyone uncomfortable by asking them to remove their shoes and yet I couldn't help wishing that they would follow my example and remove them at the door. Eventually I settled on a compromise: our family continues to remove our shoes at the door but we are once again used to having visitors wear shoes in the house.

This is only one example of the kinds of cultural "treasures" you will bring home with you. It will take time for you to decide how best to make and keep them part of your lives back in your home country.

You will also find that your interests have broadened considerably as a result of living overseas. You read different kinds of books, follow international news reports, enjoy unusual restaurants or movies. In a variety of ways you look at the world differently. Some of your old friends may find this disconcerting at first, and it will probably take some time to readjust to each other. But real friendships thrive on growth and change, and you will find with these special few that you still have a lot to share and learn from each other. In the meantime, be sure to listen as well as talk; whatever other people have been doing for the past few years is just as important to them as your activities are to you.

FAMILY ADJUSTMENT ISSUES

When the family returns from overseas, each family member resumes the functions of daily life: returning to school, work, and domestic responsibilities. Each family member has particular reentry issues to work through, and initially, one or more of you may feel like the proverbial square peg in a round hole. Children need to be reminded that no one's life has stood still while they have been away. They tend to picture their neighborhood, friends, and schools unchanged, with everyone awaiting their return. The initial weeks can be very difficult and equally disillusioning. Fads, styles, jargon, toys, rock groups, dances, and many other of the nuts and bolts of childhood are in constant flux. Children returning home from overseas sometimes feel completely out of step for a while and may be treated unmercifully by those "in the know." You can help your children by sharing with them your own feelings of awkwardness or loneliness. Encourage them to participate in a variety of activities in and out of school in order to become reacquainted with the "home" style of doing things. Remember that your children's memories of home may be far hazier than yours, and their return may feel as foreign as their initial arrival overseas. Encourage them to be as open to learning about home as they were to learning about the assignment country. They will discover that the more open and receptive they are to old friends and new acquaintances, the more quickly and easily they will be welcomed back.

Your children's return to school will require at least some degree of academic and social adjustment. After having attended school in a foreign country, they may be out of sync with the local curriculum. Through no fault of their own, they may be ahead in some subjects and behind in others. They may find themselves having to repeat subject matter that was just completed in the previous school. Conversely, children may need to be tutored in subjects which were taught differently overseas.

Teachers can also make life difficult for children returning from overseas. One little girl, who had lived for several years in France, was told by her classroom teacher that she needed to forget about France and be quiet about her past. When her parents visited the school, they were told by the principal that their daughter was back in America now and needed to be like everyone else. The parents found her a different school where she was able to readjust comfortably to American life and still be appreciated for the unique things she had to contribute to the class. An older child found that her recent, firsthand knowledge of Israel was "wrong" because it didn't match what was written in an old school textbook.

Even in the most flexible and tolerant of environments, your children will need to deemphasize some aspects of their expat life. Frequent references to exotic vacations, maids, drivers, or country clubs will not be appreciated. Young children may not even be aware of the impression they are making when they talk about their experience. Imagine a family in Pittsburgh who has never left the United States. Their ten-year-old son invites a new boy in class over to play after school. The mother overhears the following conversation between her son and his friend:

> Friend: Have you seen the show *Cats*?
> Son: Are you kidding? Have you?
> Friend: Yeah. I saw it in London, or maybe it was Australia. I get those two mixed up.

Overall, remember that the overseas assignment has been an invaluable educational experience for your children, the effects of which will last far longer than the temporary resettlement pains. Reassure them that they are not at fault for any gaps in their knowledge and that you will provide whatever help they need to catch up with the new academic curriculum and to readjust to their home country.

Adults as well as children may think that they no longer fit well into the local scene—that their newfound talents and expertise are unappreciated and underutilized. It is common to find that their employers do not yet value overseas experience, particularly if the top management personnel have not themselves been overseas. Thus, expatriates return home having learned a variety of new skills and having been exposed to different ideas and ways of doing business, none of which are deemed relevant in their new jobs. Furthermore, they may leave a position of authority and independence only to return home to a new job with less autonomy and control. The experience gained overseas seems to exist in a vacuum, unrelated to past or future work. Companies and organizations are gradually becoming more sophisticated in their overseas operations as the pressures of foreign trade expand. Personnel with overseas experience and expertise will be assuming greater importance and receiving greater recognition. In the meantime, however, many employees find returning to the home office to be frustrating, disappointing, and often boring. You may want to consider the possibility of looking for other job opportunities which make greater use of your new skills.

Whatever your decision, remember that the knowledge you have gained is now part of you and will enhance any work you do, either in your present company or elsewhere.

Women who have developed new interests and skills while overseas may also have difficulty finding ways in which to utilize them. Women who attempt to share a foreign language, cooking, or crafts, for example, are sometimes seen by others as trying to show off or be different. The fact is, of course, that people returning home have changed in some ways and *are* different. When others deny or devalue the things you have learned, it may begin to feel as though the time spent overseas had no meaning, that it was a chunk taken out of your life rather than a new dimension added to it. With some effort and perseverance, you can sidestep some of this problem. Continue to share your new interests and skills with your family and enthusiastic friends (there will be at least one or two!). At the same time, begin to explore your area for appropriate outlets for your energies. Examples of these might include the following: international organizations; adult education courses in history, literature, language, or art; courses in foreign crafts; museums and art galleries; programs in cross-cultural studies.

If none of the above are available where you live, think about the possibility of starting something on your own. Consider becoming a host family for foreign students attending nearby colleges; later you might even want to have a high school exchange student for a year. Some classroom teachers are delighted to find parents willing to give talks on cross-cultural topics. If your local school and church have foreign families in them, you may be able to initiate a cross-cultural program which offers children (and their parents) an opportunity to experience various aspects of different cultures and make new friends. A woman returning to Ridgewood, New Jersey, found that her daughter's class of twenty included children from India, Korea, Colombia, Romania, Germany, and Israel. As with each previous step of your overseas assignment, you must identify your available options and choose those which best enable you to pursue your new interests.

Women returning to the work force or to their own professional careers face problems similar to those experienced by any women who return to work after an extended time away. Chances are that some improvements have taken place in your absence that may make things easier for you, so it is important to look carefully into the local employment scene. Corporate day-care facilities and maternity/paternity leaves are examples of the kinds of changes which have recently begun to take place as a result of the gradual redefining of women's roles.

Explain your time away from the job market in a positive way, emphasizing the benefits you have gained from your experience. Think creatively about what you have to offer. If you need retraining because your chosen field has moved ahead without you, this is an ideal time to take brushup courses. If you want to enter a new field, use this opportunity to go back to school.

You may find in moments of frustration that you start to resent the time spent on assignment (or even your husband for having interrupted your life and career). This would mean, however, that you are also denying and devaluing your experiences overseas. Whatever happens on your return home, it is important to see this next period in your life as an outgrowth or development of everything that has gone before. What you have learned or gained from your time overseas will add immeasurably to what comes next.

"You can't go home again," Thomas Wolfe said. As former expats will attest, the return is indeed difficult for all members of the family. The home you come back to is different from the one you left, even if they are one and the same. Every member of the family has changed; each of you is older and at a different point in your life. The world as you know it has both grown and shrunk. It includes countries, peoples, governments, and cultures which previously meant little or nothing to you, yet you have formed friendships and bonds which span oceans and national boundaries.

Just as the expectations you took overseas caused discomfort when they were not met by your new cultural environment, so the expectations you bring home may not be met by your home environment. These may be the expectations of home being the ideal place you have dreamed of it being while you were away or the expectation that people at home will be exactly the same as before you left. As a result, you may find yourself having the same culture shock experiences you had overseas in response to these kinds of disappointed expectations—withdrawal, irritation, fatigue, insomnia, or temporary depression.

At times during the initial months of reentry, the sense of discomfort, alienation, and awkwardness will seem overwhelming. You may wish that you had never come home or even that you had never dared to leave in the first place. In your family discussions, try to remember that this reentry phase of your lives is temporary. By utilizing the same energy, humor, and determination which helped you through the adjustment to expat life, you will make it over this final hurdle. You will still have the friends and the memories from your years overseas long after the anxiety and stress of your return have finally receded into the past. You will have added to your own lives an exciting dimension that can never be taken away.

Recommended Readings

FOR ADULTS

The Art of Crossing Cultures. Craig Storti. Yarmouth, ME: Intercultural Press, 1990. A valuable and readable discussion of the process of adapting to and enjoying a culture that differs from your own.

Breaking the Language Barrier. H. Douglas Brown. Yarmouth, ME: Intercultural Press, 1991. The author leads the reader through a series of steps designed to help the reader identify his or her unique language-learning style. Combines a sophisticated analysis of the language-learning process with practical guidelines for readers.

Bringing Up Children Overseas. Sidney Werkman. New York: Basic Books, 1977. An in-depth discussion of the challenges of parenting overseas.

Cross-Cultural Reentry. Clyde N. Austin, ed. Abilene, TX: Abilene Christian University Press, 1986. A book of articles on reentry issues. Three groups are targeted: government employees, business and missionary families and international students, and third-culture children (and parents). Includes exercises.

Did Somebody Pack the Baby. Barbara Friedrich and Sally Hulstrand. Englewood Cliffs, NJ: Prentice-Hall, 1978. Although written primarily as a how-to manual for domestic moves, the suggestions, timetables, and checklists are still quite useful.

Grow Your Roots Anywhere, Anytime. Ronald J. Raymond, Jr. and Stephen J. Eliot. Ridgefield, CT: Peter H. Wyden, Inc., 1980. Written by two psychologists about corporate domestic moves, this book should be read by any family moving anywhere.

Moving Abroad. Virginia McKay. Wilmington, DE: VLM Enterprises, 1982. An excellent how-to manual for overseas moves that will take you through the step-by-step process of relocating. Available from VLM Enterprises, P.O. Box 7236, Wilmington, DE 19803.

Survival Kit for Overseas Living—For Americans Planning to Live and Work Abroad. L. Robert Kohls. Yarmouth, ME: Intercultural Press, 1996. Examines the impact of differences in perceptions, values and behavior on the overseas sojourn and recommends ways to respond positively to the experience. Suggested reading for anyone going abroad, for the first or the twentieth time.

The Whole World Guide to Language Learning. Terry Marshall. Yarmouth, ME: Intercultural Press, 1990. Community-based, individualized guide to learning language. Central to the technique is a native-speaking mentor and a lesson format called the "daily learning cycle."

Women's Guide to Overseas Living. Barbara Hornby and Nancy Piet-Pelon. Yarmouth, ME: Intercultural Press, 1992. This revised edition of the popular *In Another Dimension* includes new chapters on culture shock, reentry, and special concerns.

Women on the Move—A Christian Perspective on Cross-Cultural Adaptation. Gretchen Janssen. Yarmouth, ME Intercultural Press, 1992. Formerly entitled *Women Overseas,* this book is a guide for women who wish to tap the strength of their religious convictions in dealing with the stresses of cross-cultural adaptation. Includes exercises.

FOR CHILDREN

Ages 3–6:

Anno's Counting House. Mitsumasa Anno. New York: Philomel, 1982. A delightful picture book showing the gradual move of possessions and people from one house to another.

Moving. Fred Rogers. New York: Putnam, 1987. Color photographs accompany Mr. Rogers's reassuring description of the moving process.

Moving Day. Tobi Tobias. New York: Knopf, 1976. A small girl helps her teddy bear through the process of moving from their old house to a new house.

Moving Molly. Shirley Hughes. New York: Lothrop, 1988. Describes Molly's loneliness following her family's move from the city to the country.

Ages 5–10:

Gila Monsters Meet You at the Airport. Marjorie Sharmot. Palmer, AR: Aladdin Books, 1980. Ages 5–7. A young boy moving out west and a young boy moving back east share their misconceptions about their new homes. An amusing story which will help to elicit children's fears and concerns about the new country.

Goodbye, House—A Kid's Guide to Moving. Ann Banks and Nancy Evans. New York: Harmony Books, 1980. Ages 5–10. A wonderful activity book and secret diary for children experiencing a move.

Home Is Where My Heart Lives: A Workbook for Children on the Move. Available from the National Childhood Grief Institute, 3300 Edinborough Way, Suite 512, Minneapolis, MN 55435. A cheerful and creative way for children to draw and talk about moving.

I'm Moving. Martha Hickman. Nashville, TN: Abingdon, 1974. Ages 5–8. A story dealing with what you take and what you leave behind when you move, what is the same and what is different about your new home.

Maggie Doesn't Want to Move. Elizabeth O'Donnell. New York: Four Winds Press, 1987. Ages 6–10. A lovely story about an older brother who describes his own worries and concerns by attributing them to his little sister.

The Monster in the Third Dresser Drawer and Other Stories about Adam Joshua. Janice Smith. New York: Harper Collins, 1988. Ages 5–7. In a chapter entitled "The Terrible Move," a young boy's unhappiness over his family's move is described with humor and understanding.

A Smooth Move. Berniece Rabe. New York: Bradbury, 1988. Ages 5–7. A young boy keeps a journal about his move from Oregon to Washington, D.C., and describes aspects of moving which include the moving men, the trip, and motel living.

Middle School:

Hedgehogs in the Closet. Joan Carris. New York: Lippincott, 1988. A story about a 14-year-old boy's move to England because of his father's job.

Murphy's Island. Colleen O'Shaughnessy. New York: Scholastic, 1990. A story about a sixth-grade girl's short-term move to a new home and the social problems she encounters and solves in her new school.

This Place Has No Atmosphere. Paula Danziger. New York: Delacorte, 1986. A fifteen-year-old girl moves with her parents to the moon in the year 2057.

Teenagers:

Help! We're Moving. Dianna Booher. New York: J. Messner, 1983. A how-to book on moving for teenagers which includes a chapter on overseas moves.

The Teenager's Survival Guide to Moving. Patricia Cooney Nida and Wende M. Heller. New York: Atheneum, 1985. A how-to book on moving for teenagers.